A Handbook of Microeconomics

Theory and Applications

A Handbook of Microeconomics

Theory and Applications

Pankaj Gupta

CYBER TECH PUBLICATIONS

4264/3, Ansari Road, Daryaganj New Delhi - 110002

Phone : 011-43559448, Fax : 011-23280028

Email : cybertechpublications@gmail.com

A Handbook of Microeconomics Theory and Applications
CYBER TECH PUBLICATIONS
4264/3, Ansari Road, Daryaganj
New Delhi - 110002.(India)
Phone : 011-23244078, 011-43559448,
Fax : 011-23280028
E-mail : cybertechpublications@gmail.com
Website : www.cybertechpublications.com

First Published : 2008

ISBN 978-81-7884-358-2

Price,750/

Printed at :

New Green Print Solutions, New Delhi 110078

Contents

Preface

'Macroeconomics' is a branch of economics dealing with the performance, structure, behavior and decision-making of the entire economy. This includes a national, regional, or global economy. With microeconomics, macroeconomics is one of the two most general fields in economics.

Infact, macroeconomists study aggregated indicators such as GDP, unemployment rates, and price indices to understand how the whole economy functions. Macroeconomists develop models that explain the relationship between such factors as national income, output, consumption, unemployment, inflation, savings, investment, international trade and international finance. In contrast, microeconomics is primarily focused on the actions of individual agents, such as firms and consumers, and how their behavior determines prices and quantities in specific markets.

It is pertinent to note that while macroeconomics is a broad field of study, there are two areas of research that are emblematic of the discipline: the attempt to understand the causes and consequences of short-run fluctuations in national income (the business cycle), and the attempt to understand the determinants of long-run economic growth (increases in national income).

Remarkably, macroeconomic models and their forecasts are used by both governments and large corporations to assist in the development and evaluation of economic policy and business strategy.

The present book is devised as a standard reference work on macroeconomics. All salient features of macroeconomics are suitable addressed. The entire gamut of information consists of following main chapters—Introduction; Macroeconomic Thought: A Historical Overview; Austrian Business Cycle Theory; Supply-Side Economics; Inflation; Recession; Unemployment; Monetary and Fiscal Policy; Role of Central Bank; Glossary and Bibliography etc.

Students, researchers and teachers of economics will find this informative and useful. Simultaneously different aspirants, appearing for various competitive examinations will find this equally useful.

As is obvious such works cannot be devised solely. Hence we have consulted a number of standard books, articles and websites for furnishing authoritative information. We owe gratitude to all these scholars and economists whose views and works are cited or substantially made use of in this work; their names appear in references and bibliography. However, to those whom inadertently we missed we acknowledge gratefully. My teachers, colleagues and friends have rendered whole-hearted cooperation. I am extremely grateful to them also.

Finally I am thankful my publishers for making this book superbly produced.

—Author

1

Introduction

> "A man's delight in looking forward to and hoping for some particular satisfaction is a part of the pleasure flowing out of it, enjoyed in advance. But this is afterward deducted, for the more we look forward to anything the less we enjoy it when it comes."
>
> —*Arthur Schopenhauer*

In common parlance, by 'Macroeconomics' we mean a branch of economics dealing with the performance, structure, behavior and decision-making of the entire economy. This includes a national, regional, or global economy. With microeconomics, macroeconomics is one of the two most general fields in economics.

Basically, macroeconomists study aggregated indicators such as GDP, unemployment rates, and price indices to understand how the whole economy functions. Macroeconomists develop models that explain the relationship between such factors as national income, output, consumption, unemployment, inflation, savings, investment, international trade and international finance.

In contrast, microeconomics is primarily focused on the actions of individual agents, such as firms and consumers, and how their behavior determines prices and quantities in specific markets.

It is pertinent to note that while macroeconomics is a broad field of study, there are two areas of research that are emblematic of the discipline: the attempt to understand the causes and consequences of short-run fluctuations in national income (the business cycle), and the attempt to understand the determinants of long-run economic growth (increases in national income).

Remarkably, macroeconomic models and their forecasts are used by both governments and large corporations to assist in the development and evaluation of economic policy and business strategy.

It is apt to mention that the term "macroeconomics" stems from the term "macrosystem", coined by the Norwegian economist Ragnar Frisch in 1933. It is the culmination of a long-standing effort to comprehend many of the broad elements of the field. Macroeconomic theory fused, and extended, the earlier study of business fluctuations and monetary economics.

Mark Blaug, a notable historian of economic thought, proclaimed in his "Great Economists before Keynes: 1986" that Swedish economist Knut Wicksell "more or less founded modern macroeconomics".

Various Schools of Thought

The traditional distinction is between two different approaches to economics: Keynesian economics, focusing on demand, and neoclassical economics, based on rational expectations and efficient markets. Keynesian thinkers challenge the ability of markets to be completely efficient generally arguing that prices and wages do not adjust well to economic shocks. None of the views are typically endorsed to the complete exclusion of the others, but most schools do emphasize one or the other approach as a theoretical foundation.

Keynesian Tradition

Keynesian economics is an academic theory heavily influenced by the economist John Maynard Keynes. This school focuses on aggregate demand to explain levels of unemployment and the business cycle. That is, business cycle fluctuations should be reduced through fiscal policy (the government spends more or less depending on the situation) and monetary policy. Early Keynesian macroeconomics was "activist," calling for regular use of policy to stabilize the capitalist economy, while some Keynesians called for the use of incomes policies. Important early proponents included Robert Solow, Paul Samuelson, James Tobin, and Alvin Hansen.

Neo-Keynesians combined Keynes thought with some neoclassical elements in the neoclassical synthesis. Neo-Keynesianism waned and was replaced by a new generation of models that made up New Keynesian economics, which developed partly in response to new classical economics. New Keynesianism strives to provide microeconomic foundations to Keynesian economics by showing how imperfect markets can justify demand management.

Post-Keynesian economics represents a dissent from mainstream Keynesian economics, emphasizing the importance of demand in the long run as well as the short, and the role of uncertainty.

Neoclassical Tradition

For decades Keynesians and classical economists split into autonomous areas, the former studying macroeconomics and the latter studying microeconomics. In the 1970s new classical macroeconomics challenged Keynesians to ground their macroeconomic theory in microeconomics. The main policy difference in this second stage of macroeconomics is an increased focus on monetary policy, such as interest rates and money supply. This school emerged during the 1970s with the Lucas critique. New classical macroeconomics based on rational expectations, which means that choices are made optimally considering time and uncertainty, and all markets are clearing. New classical macroeconomics is generally based on real business cycle models such as the work of Edward Prescott.

Monetarism, led by Milton Friedman, holds that inflation is always and everywhere a monetary phenomenon. It rejects fiscal policy because it leads to "crowding out" of the private sector. Further, it does not wish to combat inflation or deflation by means of active demand management as in Keynesian economics, but by means of monetary policy rules, such as keeping the rate of growth of the money supply constant over time.

To try to avoid major economic shocks, such as The Great Depression, and more recently global recession in 2010 governments make adjustments through policy changes they expect will stabilize the economy. Governments believe the success of these adjustments is necessary to maintain stability and continue growth. This economic management is achieved through two types of governmental strategies:

(a) Fiscal policy; and
(b) Monetary policy.

As we intend to elucidate all facets of macroeconomics in this book in compact form, we will take them stepwise in the succeeding chapters.

First we will illustrate macroeconomics in historical perspective.

REFERENCES

Blanchard, Olivier (2000), *Macroeconomics,* Prentice Hall.

Blaug, Mark (1986), *Great Economists before Keynes,* Brighton: Wheatsheaf.

Fengbo Zhang: *Analysis of Chinese Macroeconomy.*

Friedman, Milton (1953), *Essays in Positive Economics,* London: University of Chicago Press.

Gärtner, Manfred (2006), *Macroeconomics,* Pearson Education Limited.

Heijdra, B.J.; Ploeg, F. van der (2002), *Foundations of Modern Macroeconomics,* Oxford University Press.

Mishkin, Frederic S. (2004), *The Economics of Money, Banking, and Financial Markets,* Boston: Addison-Wesley, p. 517.

Snowdon, Brian, and Howard R. Vane, ed. (2002). An Encyclopedia of Macroeconomics, Description & scroll to Contents-preview links.

Snowdon, Brian; , Howard R. Vane (2005), *Modern Macroeconomics: Its Origins, Development And Current State,* Edward Elgar Publishing.

Warsh, David (2006), *Knowledge and the Wealth of Nations,* Norton.

2

Macroeconomic Thought: A Historical Overview

"Money spent on ourselves may be a millstone about the neck; spent on others it may give us wings like eagles."

— *Raymond Hitchcock*

First, without exaggeration, it can be admitted that modern macroeconomics can be said to have begun with John Maynard Keynes and the publication of his book The General Theory of Employment, Interest and Money in 1936. Before Keynes, economists used microeconomic methods to explain aspects of economics like employment, price level, and interest rates.

Keynes's seminal work sparked the Keynesian Revolution. He abandoned the ideas of earlier, "classical" economists who thought markets would always clear and there would be no surplus goods or labor wasted in the market.

As such, Keynes shifted the focus of many economists to the study of aggregates, such as the unemployment rate, total income and the aggregate price level and inflation.

Remarkably, a generation of economists following Keynes synthesized his theory with neoclassical microeconomics to form the neoclassical synthesis. Keynesian economics soon faced challenges from new classical macroeconomics. Milton Friedman adopted some Keynesian ideas, like the importance of the demand of money, but challenged Keynesian theories of price level and fiscal policy. Keynesian economics also faced the Lucas critique that its aggregate level view was not consistent with microeconomic theories.

Robert Lucas and other economists criticized Keynesian models that did not work under rational expectations. Finally, the new classical school developed Real Business Cycle Theory, first proposed by Finn E. Kydland and Edward C. Prescott. Like classical economic models, RBC models assume markets clear and business cycles are driven by changes in technology and supply, not demand, as Keynes proposed. New Keynesian economics tried to address many of these criticisms.

New Keynesians built models with microfoundations of sticky prices that suggested recessions could still be explained by demand factors. The new neoclassical synthesis combined elements of both new classical and new Keynesian macroeconomics to form a consensus in macroeconomics. The financial crisis and subsequent recession cast doubt on the mainstream consensus and its understanding of the macroeconomy.

Commentators have launched a variety of criticisms against the prevailing tenets of macroeconomics. The economic crisis has drawn attention to new ideas and old heterodox theories that have the potential to address problems in mainstream macroeconomics.

The Beginning

As already stated, macroeconomics descends from the two areas of research: Business cycle theory and monetary theory. Business cycle theory covered a wide range of different explanations for business cycles. Most theories focused on a single factor, which could range from weather to monetary policy. These theories presented partial pictures of the economy and never fully integrated the market for real goods with financial market for money.

At this time in monetary theory the macroeconomic relationship between price level and output was explained by the quantity theory of money. A simple version of the quantity theory can be expressed with the equation of exchange by holding the product of money supply and money velocity equivalent to nominal income (the product of real income and the price level).

This theory applied Say's law to the macroeconomy: A certain amount of goods were produced and they were sold at whatever price cleared the market. Adding more money to the system would only raise prices, not create more goods. This classical theory held that money velocity was stable and independent of economic activity. Cambridge economists, including Keynes, began to challenge this assumption.

They looked at money demand and how it impacted the the economy through the Cambridge cash balance theory and equation. While the Cambridge equation is similar to the classical equation of exchange, it does not assume money demand and supply are always at equilibrium and it accounts for people holding more cash when the economy sags.

By factoring in the value people place in holding cash itself, the Cambridge economists took significant steps toward the concept of liquidity preference in Keynes's General Theory.

The Cambridge theory argued that people would hold

money for the purposes of facilitating transactions and maintaining liquidity. Keynes's General Theory added a third motive, speculation, to his liquidity preference theory and built on it to create his general theory.

General Theory of J.M. Keynes

In fact, Keynes's *The General Theory of Employment, Interest and Money* expanded on the concept liquidity preferences and built a general theory of how the economy worked that radically broke from the classical view. Keynes's theory, the first to bring together both monetary and the real economic factors, explained unemployment and recessions, and provided a potential solution to stabilize the economy. Keynes argued that economic output was correlated with money velocity via liquidity preferences: People prefer to hold more liquidity in bad economic times and slow the exchange of money by holding on to cash.

Through liquidity preferences, Keynes attacked velocity as the weak spot of quantity theory. His theory challenged the classical view of money velocity as stable and uncorrelated with output. Moreover, it turned the quantity theory of money on its head by assuming that changes in the market would shift quantities instead of adjusting prices.

Markets—including the labor market--might not clear, leaving excess goods to waste and capacity to idle.

Here it is apt to mention that classical economists had difficulty explaining involuntary unemployment and downturns in the economy. They applied Say's Law to the labor market and expected the labor market to clear (all those willing to work at the prevailing wage would have work). Keynes challenged the classical economists' assumptions.

If the market for goods did not clear because of a lack of aggregate demand, fewer workers are needed for production and unemployment increases. In Keynes's model employment and output were driven my expenditures, the sum of consumption and investment. While, in Keynes's view, consumption stayed stable, investment violently fluctuates depending on changes in variety of factors including expectations, "animal spirits," and interest rates. Keynes argued that fiscal policy could be used to fix the situation.

If the private sector would not spend, the government could use spending to employ idle resources. Government spending could be used to employ resources that did not sell on the market including the labor of unemployed workers.

Moreover, this direct spending would be increased by the multiplier effect since newly employed workers would spend their income, which would percolate through the economy and boost aggregate demand. The exact meaning of Keynes's work has been long debated. Economists even debate the interpretation of his policy prescription for unemployment, one of the more explicit parts of The General Theory, and whether it was intended as a revolutionary reaction to a serious problem or a moderately conservative solution to deal with the issue.

These disputes covered the exact formulations, mechanisms, and consequences of the Keynesian model. One group emerged representing the "orthodox" interpretation of Keynes, and they merged classical microeconomics with Keynesian thought to produce the "neoclassical synthesis."

Neoclassical Synthesis

It is apt to mention that the generation of economists following Keynes, Neo-Keynesians, created the "neoclassical synthesis" by combining the macroeconomics of the General Theory with Walrasian microeconomics, where individual markets for goods worked together to sell all goods in a system with perfect competition, no externalities, and perfect information. The neoclassical synthesis dominated economics from the 1940s until the early 1970s. By the mid 1950s, ninety percent of economists had ceased debating Keynesianism and accepted the synthesis view. However, much of Keynes's original thought had been left out of the synthesis.

Keynes's emphasis on uncertainty and its potential to slow the economy found no place in the mainstream. The simplified Keynesian thought of the synthesis attributed problems with market clearing to slow price changes that failed to quickly adjust to changes in supply and demand.

Don Patinkin challenged the synthesis view that nominal rigidities caused unemploument and argued that inadequate demand caused unemployment even with flexible wages and prices. Pantinkin, Robert W. Clower, and Axel Leijonhufvud formed a dissenting group that criticized the dominant interpretation of Keynes and focused on the role of disequilibrium. Following in the disequilibrium tradition, Robert Barro and Herschel Grossman created formalized, general disequilibrium models.

1. Neo-Keynesian Models

In fact, John Hicks incorporated Keynes's thought into a general equilibrium framework where the markets for goods and money met in an overall equilibrium. The IS/LM model became the basis for theorizing for decades, and it was used for policy analysis into the 1960s. Other economists built on the IS/LM framework. Notably, in 1944, Franco Modigliani added a labor market with rigid nominal wages to the basic IS/LM model.

Modigliani's model represented the economy as a system with general equilibrium across the interconnected markets for labor, finance, and goods, and it explained unemployment with rigid nominal wages. Economists incorporated the theoretical work from the synthesis into large-scale macroeconometric models. Individual equations for factors such as consumption, investment, and money demand where combined into models of the economy based on many variables.

This line of research reached its height with the MIT-Penn-Social Science Research Council (MPS) model developed by Modigliani and his collaborators. The MPS model combined the elements of IS/LM with other aspects of the synthesis including Robert Solow's growth model and the Philip's curve relation between inflation and output. Both large-scale models and the Philip's curve became targets for critics of the synthesis.

2. Phillips Curve

Keynes's General Theory did not lay out an explicit theory of price level. Early Keynesian models assumed wage and other price levels were fixed. These assumptions caused little concern in the 1950s when inflation was stable, but by the mid-1960s inflation increased and became an issue for macroeconomic models.

In 1958 A.W. Phillips set the basis for a price level theory when he made the empirical observation that inflation and the unemployment rate seemed to be inversely correlated. In 1960, Lipsey provided the first theoretical explanation of this correlation. Generally Keynesian explanations of the curve held that excess demand drove high inflation and low unemployment while an output gap raised unemployment and put downward pressure on prices. In the late 1960s and early 1970s, the Phillips curve would face attacks on both empirical and theoretical fronts. The trade off between output and inflation represented by the curve was the weakest part of the Keynesian system.

Monetarism

Here it is apt to mention that Milton Friedman developed an alternative to Keynesian macroeconomics eventually labeled monetarism. Definitions of the school of thought can be loose, but generally monetarism can be thought of as the idea that money matters for the macroeconomy. When monetarism began in the 1950s and 1960s, Keynesians neglected the role money played in inflation and the business cycle, and monetarism directly challenged them on those points.

The Philips Curve and Inflation

In fact, the Philips curve appeared to be a clear, inverse relationship between inflation and output. The curve broke down in the 1970s as economies suffered stagflation, simultaneous increases in inflation and unemployment. The empirical implosion of the Philips curve followed attacks mounted on theoretical grounds by Milton Friedman and Edmund Phelps. Phelps, not a monetarist himself, argued that only unexpected inflation or deflation could impact employment.

Variations of Phelps's expectations-augmented Phillips curve remain standard tools for macroeconomists. Friedman and Phelps's work showed that there was no long-run trade off between inflation and unemployment. In their thinking, their is a natural rate of unemployment, and expansionary monetary policy can only temporarily shift unemployment below this level.

Eventually, firms will adjust their prices and wages for inflation based on real factors and the nominal changes from monetary policy will be ignored. As such the expansionary boost will be wiped out.

Anna Schwartz collaborated with Friedman to produce one of the major works of monetarism: A Monetary History of the United States (1963), a study of United States monetary history that linked money supply with the business cycle. The Keynesians of the 1950s and 60s had adopted the view that monetary policy did not impact aggregate output or the business cycle. They based this belief on evidence that, during the Great Depression, interest rates had been extremely low but output remained depressed.

Friedman and Schwartz argued that Keynesians missed the relationship by only looking at nominal interest rates and neglecting real interest rates. Real interest rates showed that borrowing had been expensive during the Depression and monetary policy had effectively been contractionary. Friedman developed his own quantity theory of money that referred back to Fisher's but inherited much from Keynes. Friedman's 1956 *"The Quantity Theory of Money: A Restatement"* incorporated Keynes's demand for money and liquidity preference into an equation similar to the classical equation of exchange. Friedman's updated quantity theory also allowed for the possibility of using monetary or fiscal policy to remedy a downturn.

Friedman broke with Keynes by arguing that money demand would be relatively stable—even during a down turn. Friedman and other monetarists argued that "fine-tuning" through fiscal and monetary policy would be counter productive. They found money demand to be stable even during fiscal policy, and both fiscal and monetary policies suffered from lags that made them too slow to react to changes in the economy.

It is significant to note that monetarism became

politically popular in the late 1970s and 1980s. Friedman and Phelps's prediction of an unstable Philips curve proved true in the face of stagflation and gave monetarism a boost in credibility. By the mid-1970s monetarism became the new orthodoxy in macroeconomics, and by the late-1970s central banks in the United Kingdom and United States adopted a monetarist policy of targeting monetary supply instead of interest rates when setting policy. Monetarism's political prominence quickly sank. To start with, targeting monetary aggregates proved difficult for central banks.

Monetarism faced a major test when Paul Volcker took over the Federal Reserve Chairmanship. Volcker used tight monetary policy to end out of control inflation; however, Volcker created a recession in the process. The recession quickly made monetarism unpopular, but, in hindsight, the "experiment" clearly demonstrated the capability of monetary policy to influence the economy.

Monetarism also became less credible when once stable money velocity defied monetarist predictions and began to move erratically in United States during the early-1980s. Monetarism waned politically, but its core tenets of long-run money neutrality and use of monetary policy for stabilization became enshrined in the macroeconomic mainstream even among present-day Keynesians.

New Classical Macroeconomics

New classical macroeconomics, sometimes simply called new classical economics, is a school of thought in macroeconomics that builds its analysis entirely on neoclassical framework. Specifically, it emphasizes the importance of rigorous foundations based on microeconomics. Macroeconomic model is built in analogy to the actions of individual agents, whose behavior is modeled in microeconomics.

New classical macroeconomics strives to provide neoclassical microeconomic foundations for macroeconomic analysis. This is in contrast with its rival new Keynesian school that uses microfoundations such as price stickiness and imperfect competition to generate macroeconomic models similar to earlier, Keynesian ones.

Classical economics was the first modern school of economics. It generally believed in the ability of the market to be self-correcting as well as being the most superior institution in allocating resources. The publication of Adam Smith's the Wealth of Nations in 1776 is considered to be the birth of the school. The marginal revolution that occurred in Europe in the 19th century later further strengthened the school with concepts that continue to be central in modern microeconomics.

Since, the classical school dominated the field up until the Great Depression and the publication of The General Theory of Employment, Interest and Money by John Maynard Keynes in 1936. Keynes proposed a new framework—now known as Keynesian school—that successfully challenged classical assumptions. Keynes believed that the market is susceptible to efficiency loss. His work marked the beginning of modern macroeconomics.

Post-War period saw the successful implementation of Keynesian economic policy. Its dominance in the field is best reflected by Milton Friedman's statement, "We are all Keynesians now".

Problems arose in the 1970s and the 1980s when stagflation occurred. The decade saw rising oil prices caused by OPEC embargo on the United States. This caused both high inflation and steep economic downturn that in turned caused unemployment. Keynesians were puzzled by the outbreak of stagflation because the original Phillips curve ruled it out. The new classical school emerged in the 1970s as a response to the failure of Keynesian economics to explain stagflation. New classical and monetarist criticisms led by Robert Lucas, Jr. and Milton Friedman respectively forced the rethinking of Keynesian economics. In particular, Lucas made the Lucas critique that casted doubt on Keynesian model. This strengthened the case for macro models to be based on microeconomics. Meanwhile, Friedman before the stagflation proposed that the Phillips curve did not exist and would fail.

He theorized of an existence of a natural rate of unemployment that contradicts then accepted relationship between inflation and unemployment rate. The stagflation of the 1970s proved him right.

After the 1970's and the apparent failure of Keynesian economics, the new classical school became the dominant school in Macroeconomics. This was captured by the fact that the new concepts and ideas which emerged from new classical economics such as rational expectations were accepted by the opposing new Keynesian school except for the fact that the latter still maintained the effectiveness of fiscal and monetary policy. Both the new classical and the new Keynesian schools now form the basis of mainstream macroeconomics.

New classical economics is based on Walrasian assumptions. All agents are assumed to maximize utility on the basis of rational expectations. At any one time, the economy is assumed to have a unique equilibrium at full employment or potential output achieved through price and wage adjustment. In other words, the market clears at all times.

New classical economics has also pioneered the use of representative agent models. Such models have recently received severe neoclassical criticism, pointing to the clear disjuncture between microeconomic behavior and macroeconomic results, as indicated by Kirman (1992), and the fallacy of composition. In some ways, this critique is akin to the Cambridge capital controversy.

Remarkably, the concept of rational expectations was originally used by John Muth, and was popularized by Lucas. One of the most famous new classical models is the real business cycle model, developed by Edward C. Prescott and Finn E. Kydland.

As such a further challenge to the Keynesian paradigm began in the mid 1970s and came from "new classical economics." New classical economics and monetarism share a basis in classical economics, and monetarism has even been labeled as the "first wave" of new classical economics. However, the new classical economists did not share the monetarist belief that monetary policy could systematically impact the economy. They also broke with Keynesian economic theory completely while the monetarists built on Keynesian ideas. Despite their disputes with the Keynesians, new classical economists did share the Keynesian focus on explaining short-run fluctuations.

When new classical economists replaced monetarists as the primary opponents to Keynesianism, they shifted the debate from whether to look at short-run fluctuations to whether macroeconomic models should be grounded in microeconomic theories. Like monetarism, new classical economics was rooted at the University of Chicago, principally with Robert Lucas, but new classical economics spread to other institutions—especially freshwater schools. Robert Barro at Harvard, and Finn Kydland at Carnegie Mellon and Edward Prescott at University of Minnesota all contributed to its development. New classical economists criticized the weak connection between Keynesian macroeconomics and microeconomic theory.

They also introduced rational expectations and doubted the ability of the government to stabilize the economy when these expectations were factored into economic models. Most controversially, new classical economists revived the market clearing assumption of the classics, implying that prices were flexible and that the market should be modeled at equilibrium.

It is apt to mention that Keynesians and monetarists recognized that people based their economic decisions on expectations of the future, but, until the 1970s most models relied on adaptive expectations, which assumed that future expectations were based on an average of past trends. For example, if the inflation rate averaged 4% over the past few years, economic agents were assumed to expect 4% inflation the next year. In 1972 Robert Lucas, influenced by a 1961 agricultural economics paper by John Muth, introduced rational expectations to macroeconomics.

Under rational expectations, expectations are based on optimal forecasts. This does not mean that people have perfect foresight, but it does mean they act with an informed understanding economic theory and policy. Essentially, adaptive expectations modeled behavior as if it were backward-looking rational expectations models economic agents who are forward-looking.

Also, an economic model would be internally inconsistent given rational expectations if it assumes that the agents it models behave as if they were unaware of the model.

Further, Thomas Sargent and Neil Wallace (1975) applied rational expectations to the Philips curve and found that monetary policy could not be used to systematically stabilze the economy. Sargent and Wallace's policy ineffectiveness proposition found that economic agents would anticipate inflation and adjust to higher price levels before the influx of monetary stimulus could boost employment and output.

Only unanticipated monetary policy could increase employment, and no central bank could systematically use monetary policy for expansion without economic agents catching on and anticipating price changes before they could have a stimulative impact. Robert E. Hall applied rational expectations to the permanent income hypothesis developed earlier by Friedman. Hall's finding implied that people will smooth their consumption over time and only alter their consumption patterns when their expectations about future income change.

The permanent income hypothesis challenged the Keynesian view that tax cuts could have a stabilizing effect. The permanent income view suggests that consumers base their spending on wealth and not income, so a temporary boost in income would only produce a moderate increase in consumption.

Empirical tests of Hall's hypothesis suggest it may understate boosts in consumption due to income increases; however, Hall's work paved the way Euler equation methods of modeling consumption that have become dominant.

The Lucas Critique and Microfoundations

It is apt to mention here that in 1976 Lucas wrote a paper criticizing large-scale Keynesian models used for forecasting and policy evaluation. Lucas argued that economic models based on empirical relationships between variables would be unstable as policies change: a relationship under one policy regime would be altered when that policy changed. The Lucas's critique went further and argued that a policy's impact would be determined by how the policy altered the expectations of economic agents.

No model could be stable unless it accounted for expectations and how expectations were related to policy. New classical economists argued that abandoning the disequlibrium models of Keynesianism and focusing on structural and behavioral based equilibrium models would remedy the faults enumerated in Lucas's critique. Keynesian economists responded to this critique by building models with microfoundations grounded in stable theoretical relationships.

Lucas and Rapping laid out the first new classical approach to aggregate supply in 1969. Under their model, changes in employment were explained based on worker preferences for leisure time. Lucas and Rapping modeled decreases in employment as voluntary choices of workers to reduce their work effort in response to the prevailing wage of the present time period. Lucas (1973) proposed a business cycle theory based on rational expectations, imperfect information, and market clearing. While building this model, Lucas attempted to incorporate the empirical fact that there had been a trade off between inflation and output without ceding that money was non-neutral in the short-run.

This model included the idea of money surprise: monetary policy only matters when it causes people to be surprised or confused about relative prices. Lucas hypothesized that producers knew what was going on in their own industries better and earlier than they did what was happening economically in other industries. Given this assumption, a producer might perceive an increase in general price level as an increase in the price of the goods he supplies.

The producer would increase his production to take advantage of increased demand only to find the "surprise" that prices had increased across the economy generally rather than specifically for his goods. Lucas's "surprise" business cycle theory fell out of favor after the 1970s and empirical evidence did not support this model. This model of business cycles has been summarized as the "Lucas supply curve," which models output as a function of the "price surprise" or the difference between expected and actual inflation.

Real Business Cycle Theory

Real business cycle theory (RBC theory) are a class of macroeconomic models in which business cycle fluctuations to a large extent can be accounted for by real (in contrast to nominal) shocks. Unlike other leading theories of the business cycle, RBC theory sees recessions and periods of economic growth as the efficient response to exogenous changes in the real economic environment.

That is, the level of national output necessarily maximizes *expected* utility, and government should therefore concentrate on the long-run structural policy changes and not intervene through discretionary fiscal or monetary policy designed to actively smooth out economic short-term fluctuations.

According to RBC theory, business cycles are therefore "real" in that they do not represent a failure of markets to clear but rather reflect the most efficient possible operation of the economy, given the structure of the economy. RBC theory differs in this way from other theories of the business cycle such as Keynesian economics and Monetarism that see recessions as the failure of some market to clear. RBC theory is associated with freshwater economics (the Chicago school of economics in the neoclassical tradition).

Business Cycles

If we were to take snapshots of an economy at different points in time, no two photos would look alike. This occurs for two reasons:

1. Many advanced economies exhibit sustained growth over time. That is, snapshots taken many years apart will most likely depict higher levels of economic activity in the later period.
2. There exist seemingly random fluctuations around this growth trend. Thus given two snapshots in time, predicting the later with the earlier is nearly impossible.

A common way to observe such behavior is by looking at a time series of an economy's output, more specifically gross national prod··ct (GNP). This is just the value of the goods and services produced by a country's businesses and workers.

While we see continuous growth of output, it is not a steady increase. There are times of faster growth and times of slower growth. A common method to obtain this trend is the Hodrick-Prescott filter. The basic idea is to find a balance between the extent to which general growth trend follows the cyclical movement (since long term growth rate is not likely to be perfectly constant) and how smooth it is. The HP filter identifies the longer term fluctuations as part of the growth trend while classifying the more jumpy fluctuations as part of the cyclical component. Observe the difference between this growth component and the jerkier data. Economists refer to these cyclical movements about the trend as business cycles. Note the horizontal axis at 0. A point on this line indicates at that year, there is no deviation from the trend. All other points above and below the line imply deviations. By using log real GNP the distance between any point and the 0 line roughly equals the percentage deviation from the long run growth trend.

We call large positive deviations (those above the 0 axis) peaks. We call relatively large negative deviations (those below the 0 axis) troughs. A series of positive deviations leading to peaks are booms and a series of negative deviations leading to troughs are recessions. At a glance, the deviations just look like a string of waves bunched together—nothing about it appears consistent. To explain causes of such fluctuations may appear rather difficult given these irregularities.

However, if we consider other macroeconomic variables, we will observe patterns in these irregularities. For example, consider fluctuations in output and consumption spending, i.e. what people buy and use at any given period. Observe how the peaks and troughs align at almost the same places and how the upturns and downturns coincide.

We might predict that other similar data may exhibit similar qualities. For example, (a) labor, hours worked (b) productivity, how effective firms use such capital or labor, (c) investment, amount of capital saved to help future endeavors, and (d) capital stock, value of machines, buildings and other equipment that help firms produce their goods.

Stylized Facts

By eyeballing the data, we can infer several regularities, sometimes called stylized facts. One is persistence. For example, if we take any point in the series above the trend, the probability the next period is still above the trend is very high. However, this persistence wears out over time. That is, economic activity in the short run is quite predictable but due to the irregular long-term nature of fluctuations, forecasting in the long run is much more difficult if not impossible.

Another regularity is cyclical variability. Column A of Table 1 lists a measure of this with standard deviations. The magnitude of fluctuations in output and hours worked are nearly equal. Consumption and productivity are similarly much smoother than output while investment fluctuates much more than output. Capital stock is the least volatile of the indicators.

it is significant to note that yet another regularity is the co-movement between output and the other macroeconomic variables. Procyclical variables have positive correlations since it usually increases during booms and decreases during recessions. Vice versa, a countercyclical variable associates with negative correlations.

Acyclical, correlations close to zero, implies no systematic relationship to the business cycle. We find that productivity is slightly procyclical. This implies workers and capital are more productive when the economy is experiencing a boom. They aren't quite as productive when the economy is experiencing a slowdown. Similar explanations follow for consumption and investment, which are strongly procyclical. Labor is also procyclical while capital stock appears acyclical. Observing these similarities yet seemingly non-deterministic fluctuations about trend, we come to the burning question of why any of this occurs. It's common sense that people prefer economic booms over recessions. It follows that if all people in the economy make optimal decisions, these fluctuations are caused by something outside the decision-making process.

So the key question really is: *what main factor influences and subsequently changes the decisions of all actors in an economy?*

Real Business Cycle Theory

Economists have come up with many ideas to answer

the above question. The one which currently dominates the academic literature on real business cycle theory was introduced by Finn E. Kydland and Edward C. Prescott in their seminal 1982 work *Time to Build And Aggregate Fluctuations*. They envisioned this factor to be technological shocks i.e., random fluctuations in the productivity level that shifted the constant growth trend up or down. Examples of such shocks include innovations, bad weather, imported oil price increase, stricter environmental and safety regulations, etc.

The general gist is that something occurs that directly changes the effectiveness of capital and/or labour. This in turn affects the decisions of workers and firms, who in turn change what they buy and produce and thus eventually affect output. RBC models predict time sequences of allocation for consumption, investment, etc. given these shocks. But exactly how do these productivity shocks cause ups and downs in economic activity? Let's consider a positive but temporary shock to productivity. This momentarily increases the effectiveness of workers and capital, allowing a given level of capital and labor to produce more output.

Notably, individuals face two types of tradeoffs. One is the consumption-investment decision. Since productivity is higher, people have more output to consume. An individual might choose to consume all of it today. But if he values future consumption, all that extra output might not be worth consuming in its entirety today.

Instead, he may consume some but invest the rest in capital to enhance production in subsequent periods and thus increase future consumption. This explains why investment spending is more volatile than consumption. The life cycle hypothesis argues that households base their consumption decisions on expected lifetime income and so they prefer to "smooth" consumption over time.

They will thus save (and invest) in periods of high income and defer consumption of this to periods of low income. The other decision is the labor-leisure tradeoff. Higher productivity encourages substitution of current work for future work since workers will earn more per hour today compared to tomorrow. More labor and less leisure results in higher output today. greater consumption and investment today.

On the other hand, there is an opposing effect: since workers are earning more, they may not want to work as much today and in future periods. However, given the pro-cyclical nature of labor, it seems that the above "substitution effect" dominates this "income effect". Overall, the basic RBC model predicts that given a temporary shock, output, consumption, investment and labor all rise above their long-term trends and hence formulate into a positive deviation. Furthermore, since more investment means more capital is available for the future, a short-lived shock may have an impact in the future.

That is, above-trend behavior may persist for some time even after the shock disappears. This capital accumulation is often referred to as an internal "propagation mechanism", since it may increase the persistence of shocks to output. It is easy to see that a string of such productivity shocks will likely result in a boom. Similarly, recessions follow a string of bad shocks to the economy. If there were no shocks, the economy would just continue following the growth trend with no business cycles. Essentially this is how the basic RBC model qualitatively explains key business cycle regularities. Yet any good model should also generate business cycles that quantitatively match the stylized facts in Table 1, our empirical benchmark. Kydland and Prescott introduced calibration techniques to do just this.

The reason why this theory is so celebrated today is

that using this methodology, the model closely mimics many business cycle properties. Yet current RBC models have not fully explained all behavior and neoclassical economists are still searching for better variations. It is important to note the main assumption in RBC theory is that individuals and firms respond optimally all the time. In other words, if the government came along and forced people to work more or less than they would have otherwise, it would most likely make people unhappy. It follows that business cycles exhibited in an economy are chosen in preference to no business cycles at all.

This is not to say that people like to be in a recession. Slumps are preceded by an undesirable productivity shock which constrains the situation. But given these new constraints, people will still achieve the best outcomes possible and markets will react efficiently. So when there is a slump, people are choosing to be in that slump because given the situation, it is the best solution. This suggests laissez-faire (non-intervention) is the best policy of government towards the economy but given the abstract nature of the model, this has been debated. A pre-cursor to RBC theory was developed by monetary economists Milton Friedman and Robert Lucas in the early 1970s. They envisioned the factor that influenced people's decisions to be misperception of wages—that booms/recessions occurred when workers perceived wages higher/lower than they really were.

This meant they worked and consumed more/less than otherwise. In a world of perfect information, there would be no booms or recessions.

Calibration

Unlike estimation, which is usually used for the construction of economic models, calibration only returns to the drawing board to change the model in the face of overwhelming evidence against the model being correct; this inverts the burden of proof away from the builder of the model. In fact, simply stated, it is the process of changing the model to fit the data. Since RBC models explain data ex post, it is very difficult to falsify any one model that could be hypothesised to explain the data. RBC models are highly sample specific, leading some to believe that they have little or no predictive power.

Structural Variables

Crucial to RBC models, "plausible values" for structural variables such as the discount rate, and the rate of capital depreciation are used in the creation of simulated variable paths. These tend to be estimated from econometric studies, with 95% confidence intervals. If the full range of possible values for these variables is used, correlation coefficients between actual and simulated paths of economic variables can shift wildly, leading some to question how successful a model which only achieves a coefficient of 80% really is.

Critical Analysis

It is apt to mention that real business cycle theory is a major point of contention within macroeconomics (Summers 1986): RBC theory categorically rejects Keynesian economics and real effectiveness of monetarism, which are the pillars of mainstream macroeconomic policy, while such noted mainstream economists as Larry Summers and Paul Krugman categorically reject RBC theory in turn:

> "(My view is that) real business cycle models of the type urged on us by [Ed] Prescott have nothing to do with the business cycle phenomena observed in the United States or other capitalist economies." –(Summers 1986)

As such, it is a common misconception that RBC theories are purely based on shocks to supply, as opposed to Keynesian theories, which are based on shocks to demand, and this leads to the common criticism of RBC theories as ignoring the demand side of the economy. However, technology-based theories of real business cycles also imply that consumers will change their intertemporal consumption and savings decisions based on the real interest rate available to them, which is a shift in demand.

Other RBC theories based on preferences implicate the demand side to an even greater extent (Plosser, 1989). Intuitively, as a market-clearing model, RBC theories do not fall clearly into either a demand-side theory or a supply-side theory as Say's law will hold in these theories and supply and demand will automatically move together.

RBC theory as avanced by Prescott, (Summers 1986) lists four:

- Prescott uses incorrect parameters (one third of household time devoted to market activity rather than one sixth; historical real interest rates of 4% rather than 1%);
- absence of independent evidence for the technology shocks that supposedly cause the business cycle, and notably being unable to point to technological causes of observed recessions;
- Prescott's models ignore prices, and its predictions on asset prices are rejected by 100 years of data by Prescott's own work;
- Prescott ignores exchange failures (e.g., failures of factories to trade their goods for workers' labor), which are central to Keynesian accounts of the causes of the Great Depression, among other crises.

In fact, a 1982 paper by Finn Kydland and Edward Prescott introduced Real Business Cycle Theory, the final wave of new classical economics. Under the theory of Kydland and Prescott, business cycles could be explained entirely by the supply-side of the economy and represented as systems at constant equilibrium. RBCT dismissed the need to incorporate price surprise, market failure, price stickiness, uncertainty, and instability into an explanation of business cycles. Kydland and Prescott built parsimonious models that explained business cycles with changes in technology and productivity that altered the desire of people to work. In contrast with economics before the 1980s, real business cycle theory radically rejected the idea of high voluntary unemployment in recessions and not only dismissed the idea that money could stabilize the economy but also the monetarist idea that money could destabilize it.

Real business cycle models were built on microfoundations of Arrow-Debreu general equilibrium and led to dynamic stochastic general equilibrium (DSGE) models. DSGE models have become a common methodological tool for macroeconomists—even those who disagree with new classical theory.

New Keynesian Economics

New classical economics had pointed out the inherent contradiction of the neoclassical synthesis: Walrasian microeconomics with market-clearing and general equilibrium could not lead to Keynesian macroeconomics where markets failed to clear. The new Keynesians recognized this paradox, but, while the new classicals abandoned Keynes, the new Keynesians abandoned Walras and market-clearing.

During the late 1970s and 1980s, new Keynesian researchers investigated how market imperfections like monopolistic competition, sticky prices and other frictions made microeconomics consistent with Keynesian macroeconomics. Despite the disagreements between the two schools, new Keynesians built much of their research on work done by the new classicals, especially by adopting rational expectations into their theory.

Stanley Fischer (1977) responded to Sargent and Wallace's monetary ineffectiveness proposition and that showed how monetary policy could stabilize an economy even in a model with rational expectations. Fischer's model showed how monetary policy could have an impact in a model with long-term, nominal wage contracts.

John B. Taylor expanded on Fischer's work and found that monetary policy could have long lasting effects—even after all wages and prices had the chance adjust. Taylor arrived at this result by building on Fischer's model with the assumptions of staggered contract negotiations and contracts that locked-in nominal prices and wage rates for extended periods.

These early new Keynesian theories were based on the basic idea that, given fixed nominal wages, a monetary authority (central bank) can control the employment rate. Since wages are fixed at a nominal rate, the monetary authority can control the real wage by changing the monetary supply and thus impact the rate of employment in the labor market. By the 1980s, new Keynesian economists became dissatisfied with these early nominal wage contract models. These models predicted that real wages would be countercyclical (real wages would rise when the economy fell), but empirical evidence showed that real wages tended to be independent of economic cycles or even slightly procyclical.

These contract models also did not make sense from an microeconomic stand point since it is unclear why firms would use long-term contracts if they led to inefficiencies. Instead of looking for the rigidities in the labor market, new Keynesians shifted their attention to the goods market and the sticky prices that resulted from menu cost models of price change. The term menu cost refers to the literal cost to a restaurant of printing new menus when it wants to change prices; however, economists also use it to refer to more general costs associated with changing prices including the expense of evaluating whether prices should be changed. Since firms have to spend money to change prices, they do not always adjust them to the point where markets clear, and this lack of price adjustments can explain why the economy may be in disequilibrium. Recent studies using data from the United States Consumer Price Index confirm that prices do tend to be sticky. A good's price typically changes about every four to six month or, if sales are excluded, every eight to eleven months. While some studies have suggested that menu costs are too small to have much of an aggregate impact, Ball and Romer (1990) showed that real rigidities could interact with nominal rigidities to create significant disequilibrium issues.

Since real rigidities keep wages high, firms must offset the cost of labor and they face another cost, on top of menu costs, that prevents them from cutting prices to a market clearing level.

Further, coordination failure is another potential explanation for recessions and unemployment. In recessions a factory can go idle even though there are people willing to work in it, and people willing to buy its production if they had jobs. In such a scenario, economic downturns appear to be the result of coordination failure: The invisible hand has failed to coordinate the usual, and optimal, flow of production and consumption. Coordination failure is an alternative to the Neo-Keynesian and classical view that downturns exist because prices do not drop fast enough in response to falling demand.

Russell Cooper and Andrew John expressed a general

form of coordination as models with multiple equilibria where agents could coordinate to improve (or at least not harm) each of their respective situations. Cooper and John based their work on earlier models including nobel laureate Peter Diamond's coconut model, which demonstrated a case of coordination failure involving search and matching theory.

In Diamond's model producer's are more likely to produce if they see others producing. The increase in possible trading partners increases the likelihood of a given producer finding someone to trade with. As in other cases of coordination failure, Diamond's model has multiple equilibria, and the welfare of one agent is dependent on the decisions of others. Diamond's model is an example of a "thick-market externality" that causes markets to function better when more people and firms participate in them. Other potential sources of coordination failure include self-fulfilling prophecies.

If a firm anticipates a fall in demand, they might cut back on hiring. A lack of job vacancies might worry workers who then cut back on their consumption. This fall in demand meets the firm's expectations, but it is entirely due to the firm's own actions.

Involuntary Unemployment

It is pertinent to note that New Keynesians explained the failure of the labor market to clear. In a Walrasian market, unemployed workers would bid down wages until the demand for workers met the supply. If markets function in the Walrasian way, unemployment would largely be illusory. The ranks of the unemployed would be limited to workers transitioning between jobs and workers who choose not to work because wages are too low to pull them into the labor market. Economists developed several theories explaining why markets might not clear leaving willing workers to waste.

Of these theories, New Keynesians were especially associated with efficiency wages and the insider-outsider model used to explain hysteresis. In efficiency wage models workers are paid at levels that maximize productivity instead of clearing the market. For example, in developing countries, firms might be able to hire workers at cut rate wages but they pay more than that rate to ensure their workers can afford enough nutrition to be productive in the workplace. Firms might also pay higher wages to increase employee loyalty. Higher morale can lead to better productivity.

Firms can also pay higher than market-clearing wages to avoid shirking. Shirking models, including one presented by Carl Shapiro and Joseph Stiglitz, were particularly influential. Shapiro and Stiglitz created a model where employees tend to shirk unless firms can monitor worker effort and threaten slacking employees with unemployment. If the economy were at full employment, a fired worker would simply move on to a new job.

A shirking worker would not be too concerned about being caught. In an economy with a reserve army of unemployed, workers worry that they will be out of a job if they are caught shirking. Keeping wages above market clearing levels creates a serious disincentive to shirk that makes workers more inefficient even though it leaves some willing workers unemployed. Economists became interested in hysteresis when unemployment levels spiked with the 1979 oil shock and early 1980s recessions but did not return to the lower levels that had been considered the natural rate.

Olivier Blanchard and Lawrence Summers explained hysteresis in unemployment with an insider-outsider model.

Insiders, employees already working at a firm, are only concerned about their own welfare. They would rather keep their wages high than cut pay and expand employment. The unemployed, outsiders, do not have any voice in the wage bargaining process, so their interests are not represented. When unemployment increases, the number of outsiders increases as well. Even after the economy has recovered, outsiders continue to be disenfranchised from the bargaining process.

The larger pool of outsiders created by periods of economic retraction can lead to persistently higher levels of unemployment. The presence of hysteresis in the labor market also raises the importance of monetary and fiscal policy. If temporary downturns in the economy can create long term increases in unemployment, stabilization policies do more than provide temporary relief; they prevent short term shocks from becoming long term increases in unemployment.

New Growth Theory

It is pertinent to note that for much of its history, macroeconomics has focused on short-run fluctuation instead of long-run economic growth. Growth had been of interest to clasical economists, but work on the topic tapered off during the marginalist revolution. The study of growth was revived when Neo-Keynesian economists developed the Harrod-Domar model that dominated growth theory until the neoclassical growth model developed by Robert Solow and Trevor Swan.

Research on the topic basically went dormant from 1970 until 1985. Papers by Paul Romer were particularly influential in igniting the growth research revival. Beginning in the mid 1980s and booming in the early 1990s many macroeconomists shifted their focus to researching the long-run and started "new growth" or endogenous growth theory. The reasons for the renaissance in growth theory are varied.

Growth economists sought to explain emprical facts including the failure of sub-Saharan countries to catch up in growth, the booming growth in the East Asian Tigers, and the slow down in productivity growth in the United States prior to the technology boom.

Also, younger economists wanted to avoid the acrimonious debate between new classicals and new Keynesians over short-run phenomena. Three different new growth models challenged neo-classical models. The first challenged the assumption of diminishing marginal returns to capital by introducing positive externalities to capital accumulation. In these models, if one firm invested in technology, there were spillover benefits to other firms because knowledge spread.

The second saw technological growth as endogenous, so entrepreneurs would be more likely to expand knowledge given more of an incentive to profit. A third set of models in new growth theory expanded the definition of capital in exogenous growth theory to include human capital. The final set of models has been labeled a "neoclassical revival" and was distinct from the first two, core models of endogenous growth theory. Endogenous growth theories implied that countries could experience rapid "catch-up" growth through an open society that encoruaged the inflow of technology and ideas from more developed nations.

Endogenous growth theory also suggests that governments should intervene to encourage investment in research and development because the private sector may not invest at optimal levels.

Further, a new consensus, called the "new neoclassical synthesis" or simply "new synthesis," has emerged in macroeconomics. The synthesis unites elements of the new Keynesian and new classical schools. The synthesis takes the methodology behind real business cycle models and combines it with the nominal rigidities (price stickiness) of new Keynesian thought. Under the synthesis the ideological underpinnings of macroeconomic research are less apparent. Regardless of school of thought, research generally concerns the impact of market imperfections on macroeconomic models.

The new synthesis has gone beyond academia and become the basis for much of the world's monetary policy. The new synthesis has united the theoretical elements of rational expectations from new classical economics with the costly price changes that produce rigidities in new Keynesian economics. Since both new classical and new Keynesian research focused on developing microfoundations, new synthesis models could be created that combined elements from both schools into a larger model.

These elements were combined in a RBC methodology called dynamic stochastic general equilibrium (DSGE) models. DSGE models arose out of attempts to develop models that did not suffer from the Lucas critique. They were based on microfoundations of firm and household behavior and preferences. They integrated these foundations in a general equilibrium framework that modeled a complete economy that tended toward equilibrium.

These models also include a "stochastic" element created by shocks to the economy. In the original RBC models these shocks were limited to technological change, but more recent models have incorporated other real changes to the economy. The union of theory and methodology has led to several empirical developments. Aspects of monetarist, Keynesian, and new classical thought have been undermined. DSGE models have shown that real, not just monetary, factors can affect the economy.

A paper by Smets and Woulters (2007) showed that monetary policy only explained a small part of the fluctuations in economic output. Along with scathing a monetarist tenet, the synthesis cast doubt on the old Keynesian idea that business cycles were entirely demand driven. In new synthesis models, disturbances to the economy can affect both demand and supply. The new synthesis also implies that monetary policy can have a stabilizing effect on the economy, contrary to new classical theory.

Issues of Financial Crisis, Recession, and the Breakdown of Consensus

The 2007-2010 financial crisis and subsequent recession has put strain on current macroeconomic theory. Few economists predicted the crisis, and, even after the crisis hit, there was no agreement on how to address it. Many people, even mainstream economists, agree that the crisis stems from an economic bubble, but neither of the major macroeconomic schools has paid much attention to finance or a theory of asset bubbles: how they form, how they can be recognized, and how they can be stopped.

The failures of current economic theory to deal with the crisis spurred many economists to reevaluate the extent of macroeconomic theory's progress. Commentary has ridiculed the mainstream and proposed adopting new ideas, reevaluating old ones, and taking a second look at what was dismissed as heterodox. DSGE models have received a good deal of criticism after the financial crisis. John Quiggin criticized them in Foreign Policy as models that put theories of optimizing and rational behavior ahead of the "observable realities" of "booms and slumps" resulting in theoretical tools that contributed nothing to the discussion of policies needed to respond to the crisis. Robert Solow took his criticism to the US Congress and testified that DSGE models had "nothing useful to say about antirecession policy" because the conclusion that macroeconomic policy is impotent is built into the "essentially implausible assumptions" behind the model. Solow also criticized one of the core assumptions of DSGE modeling, that a single, "representative agent" can represent the complex interaction of the many diverse agents that make up real world economy. Robert Gordon extended his criticism more broadly to all post-1978 macroeconomics. Gordon called for a return to non-market clearing models like those of the late 1970s. He criticized both new classical and new Keynesian economists who adopted market clearing assumptions and proposed a conception of the economy that mixed goods that followed auction-like, market clearing pricing schemes (like oil) with goods whose prices tended to be more sticky (like general consumer items).

While also condemning DSGE models Ricardo J. Caballero, offered a more positive view of modern macroeconomics by pointing to work valuable work on finance that has been done on the periphery of macroeconomics. In Caballero's view, modern macroeconomics needs to be re-centered but not scrapped completely. More radical changes to macroeconomics have been suggested. Some have advocated agent-based models (ABMs) as one potential avenue of macroeconomic research. Unlike mainstream models, ABMs do not assume the economy can achieve equilibrium and "representative agents" are replaced by agents with diverse, dynamic, and interdependent behavior including herding. ABMs take a "bottom-up" approach and can generate extremely complex and volatile simulated economies.

Where DSGE models deal with fluctuations around a stable economy, ABMs can represent unstable systems with crashes and booms that develop out of non-linear responses to proportionally small changes in the economy. A July 2010 article in The Economist looked at ABMs as alternatives to the DGSE models. The journal Nature also encouraged agent-based modeling with an editorial that suggested ABMs can do a better job of representing financial markets and other economic complexities than standard economic models.

The same issue of Nature included an essay by J. Doyne Farmer and Duncan Foley that argued ABMs could fulfill both the desires of Keynes to represent a complex economy and of Robert Lucas to construct models based on microfoundations. Farmer and Foley pointed to progress that has been made using ABMs to model parts of an economy, but argued that a very large model that incorporates low level models needs to be constructed.

Post-Keynesian Economics

While Neo-Keynesians integrated Keynes's ideas with Neoclassical theory, the Post Keynesian established a heterodox branch of Keynesianism. A loose grouping of Post Keynesians can made by splitting them into two groups: "European," including Richard Kahn, Nicholas Kaldor, Michal Kalecki, Joan Robinson, and Piero Sraffa, and "American," including Hyman Minsky, George Shackle, Sidney Weintraub, and Paul Davidson. The term "Post-Keynesian" covers a broad swath of beliefs, but Post Keynesians share at their most general level an opposition to the neoclassical synthesis and a fundamentalist interpretation of Keynes that seeks to purify economics of classical elements.

The core of narrowly defined Post Keynesian belief

can be seen as the rejection of three axioms that are central to the classical and mainstream Keynesian views of the economy: the neutrality of money, gross substitution, and the ergodic axiom. Post Keynesians not only reject the neutrality of money in the short-run, they also see money as an important factor in the long-run, a view other Keynesians dropped in the 1970s. Gross substitution implies that goods are interchangeable. If relative prices change (if the price of one good goes up, and another down) people will shift their consumption proportionally based on price.

The ergodic axiom asserts that the future of the economy can be predicted based on the past and present market conditions. Without the ergodic assumption, agents would not be able to form rational expectations and the new classical theory would be undermined. In an non-ergodic economy, predictions are very hard to make and decision making his hampered by a great deal of uncertainty. Partly because of uncertainty, Post Keynesians take a different stance sticky prices and wages than new Keynesians.

They do not see nominal rigidities as an explanation for the failure of markets to clear, in fact, Post Keynesians think sticky prices and long-term contracts can help anchor expectations and alleviate the uncertainty that hinders efficient markets. Post Keynesian economic policies emphasize the need to reduce uncertainty in the economy including safety nets and price stability.

Hyman Minsky applied Post Keynesian notions of uncertainty and instability to a theory of financial crisis where investors increasingly take on debt until their returns can no longer payoff the interest they owe on leveraged assets, resulting in a financial crisis. The financial crisis of 2007-2010 has brought mainstream attention to Minsky's work.

Austrian Business Cycle Theory

Austrian economics is generally focused on microeconomics, but Friedrich Hayek combined the capital theory of Carl Menger and Ludwig von Mises's theory of money and credit to create the Austrian business cycle theory. The Austrian business cycle starts with a model of inter-temporal capital where decisions to take the initial steps to produce a good are made long before the finished product is completed. Under this model, producers can make changes in production to adapt to changes in preferences even in the middle of the production process. In the Austrian model, producers respond to "derived demand" instead of current demand.

If consumers scale back consumption, producers assume consumers will save for additional spending later, so production will be increased to meet future demand. Combining this theory of capital production with, an economy's production possibilities frontier, and a market for loanable funds, which relates savings to investment through the interest rate, leads to a model of the macroeconomy where market mechanisms reflect intertemporal preferences.

Given this model, Austrians argue that a boom and bust cycle is initiated when a central bank cuts interest rates below the market or "natural" rate. Cheap credit initiates a boom where resources are misallocated so that early stages of production receive more resources than they should and over production begins.

Meanwhile later stages of capital are not funded for maintenance to prevent depreciation. Overproduction in the early stages cannot be processed by poorly maintained later stage capital. The boom becomes a bust and a lack of finished goods leads to "forced saving" since fewer finished goods can be produced for sale. Recovery follows the bust as capital allocation moves back to an efficient allocation. Austrian economics differs from the mainstream in many ways. Like monetarists and classicals, Austrians oppose expansionary monetary policies, but for a different reason. In the Austrian model, inflation is only a secondary problem stemming from monetary expansion, the misallocation of capital is the primary concern. Austrians criticize both mainstream schools of thought for their models of investment.

Austrians argue that classical quantity theorists ignore the difference between consumption and investment spending, and Keynesians assume investment and consumption are positively correlated with each other when Austrian theory represents them as inversely correlated with an increase in one leading to a decrease in the other.

Stockholm School

The Stockholm school, or *Stockholmsskolan*, is a school of economic thought. It refers to a loosely organized group of Swedish economists that worked together, in Stockholm, Sweden primarily in the 1930s. The Stockholm school had at the same time as John Maynard Keynes, but independently, come to the same conclusions in macroeconomics and the theories of demand and supply. Like Keynes, they were inspired by the works of Knut Wicksell, a Swedish economist active in the early years of the twentieth century.

Two of the most prominent members of the Stockholm school were Stockholm School of Economics professors Gunnar Myrdal and Bertil Ohlin. The movement's name, "The Stockholm School", was launched in an article by Bertil Ohlin in the influential *Economic Journal* in 1937, "Some Notes on the Stockholm Theory of Savings and Investment".

The article was published in response to the publication of Keynes' magnum opus, *The General Theory of Employment, Interest and Money* in 1936, and its purpose was to draw international attention to the Swedish discoveries in the field, many of which had predated the discoveries of Keynes. Gunnar Myrdal was early in supporting the theses of John Maynard Keynes, maintaining that the basic idea of adjusting national budgets to slow or speed an economy was first developed in Sweden by him and the Stockholm school.

In fact, Myrdal and Ohlin went on to further develop their theories, and in so doing they developed the intellectual underpinnings of the modern north European welfare state. Their theories were embraced and implemented as national policy by the two powerful arms of the Swedish labor movement, the Swedish Social Democratic Party and the national labor union, the Swedish Trade Union Confederation. In the post-World War II geopolitical situation, with two rival predatory political blocks, their theories also achieved wide international appeal as a "third way", i.e. a middle way between a capitalist economy and a socialist economy. The objective of this "third way" was to achieve a high level of social equality without undermining economic efficiency.

Notable Members

- Stockholm School of Economics, and later Stockholm University, professor, Gunnar Myrdal, spent many years in the U.S. writing the book *An American Dilemma: The Negro Problem and Modern Democracy*, an investigation into the situation of African Americans, funded by the Carnegie Foundation. Myrdal co-authored, together with his wife Alva Myrdal the book Crisis of the Population Question, published in 1934. The book served as a major source of inspiration for the construction of the modern Swedish welfare state, relying heavily on government intervention and social engineering to create a "people's home" (Swedish: "Folkhemmet"). The work was later criticized for its discussion of racial issues. Myrdal received the Bank of Sweden Prize in Economic Sciences in Memory of Alfred Nobel (commonly known as the "Nobel Prize for Economics") in 1974.

- Stockholm School of Economics professor Bertil Ohlin was party leader of the Swedish Liberal People's Party, the largest opposition party in the Swedish Parliament, for over twenty years (1944–1967) battling the powerful incumbent Social Democratic government. Professor Ohlin developed, together with professor Eli Heckscher, the world-wide standard economic model of international trade, the *Heckscher-Ohlin theory*. Ohlin received the Bank of Sweden Prize in 1977.
- Gustav Cassel, professor of economics at the Stockholm University, created the standard mathematical formulation of purchasing power parity, a central concept in microeconomics.
- Dag Hammarskjöld, economist. Second Secretary-General of the United Nations. In office 10 April 1953 – 18 September 1961 (when he died in a plane crash on a peacekeeping mission to the Republic of the Congo (Léopoldville)). Dag Hammarskjöld is the only person to have been awarded the Nobel Peace Prize posthumously (Alfred Nobel's testament explicitly states that the prize should be awarded only to the living).

Other members, such as Erik Lundberg, continued as business cycle-oriented economists.

REFERENCES

Barro, Robert J. (1989). "New Classicals and Keynesians, or the Good Guys and the Bad Guys". *Swiss Journal of Economics and Statistics* 125 (3): 263–273. http://www.sjes.ch/papers/1989-III-7.pdf

Beaud, Michel; Dostaler, Gilles (1997). *Economic Thought since Keynes.* New York: Routledge.

Blanchard, Olivier (2000). "What Do We Know About Macroeconomics That Fisher and Wicksell Did Not?". *Quarterly Journal of Economics* 115 (4): 1375-1409.

Blinder, Alan S. (2008). "Keynesian Economics". Concise Encyclopedia of Economics. Library of Economics and Liberty. http://www.econlib.org/library/Enc/KeynesianEconomics.html. Retrieved 25 September 2008.

Buchholz, Todd G.; Feldstein, Martin (1999). *New Ideas from Dead Economists: An Introduction to Modern Economic Thought.* New York, New York: Plume.

Caballero, Ricardo J. (27 September 2010). "Macroeconomics after the Crisis: Time to Deal with the Pretense-of-Knowledge Syndrome". MIT Department of Economics Working Paper No. 10-16.

Case, Karl E.; Ray C. Fair (2006). *Principles of Economics.* Englewood Cliffs: Prentice Hall.

Cooley, Thomas F. (1995). *Frontiers of Business Cycle Research.* Princeton: Princeton University Press.

Davidson, Paul (2003). *Financial Markets, Money and the Real World. Aldershot:* Edward Elgar Pub.

Davidson, Paul (2005). "The Post Keynesian school". In Snowdon, Brian; Vane, Howard R. *Modern Macroeconomics.* Cheltenham: E. Elgar. pp. 451-473.

Delong, J. Bradford (2000). "The Triumph of Monetarism?". The Journal of Economic Perspectives, (American Economic Association) 14 (1): 83-84.

Farmer, J. Doyne; Foley, Duncan (6 August 2009). Nature. 460. pp. 685-686.

Fletcher, Gordon (2002). "Neoclassical Synthesis". In Snowdon, Brian; Vane, Howard. *An Encyclopedia of Macroeconomics.* Northhampton, Massachusetts: Edward Elgar Publishing. pp. 522-525.

Froyen, Richard (1990). *Macroeconomics, Theories and Policies* (3rd ed.). New York: Macmillan.

Gali, Jordi (2008). *Monetary Policy, Inflation, and the Business Cycle.* Princeton: Princeton University Press.

Garrison, Roger W. (2005). "The Austrian School". In Snowdon, Brian; Vane, Howard R.. *Modern Macroeconomics.* Cheltenham: E. Elgar. pp. 474-516.

Gomes, Joao; Greenwood, Jeremy; Rebelo, Sergio (2001). "Equilibrium Unemployment". *Journal of Monetary Economics* 48 (1): 109–152.

Goodfriend, Marvin; King, Robert G. (1997). "The New Neoclassical Synthesis and the Role of Monetary Policy". *NBER Macroeconomics Annual* 12: 231-283.

Hansen, Gary D. (1985). "Indivisible labor and the business cycle". *Journal of Monetary Economics* 16 (3): 309–327.

Hoover, Kevin (2008). "New Classical Macroeconomics". The Concise Encyclopedia of Economics. Library of Economics and Liberty. http://www.econlib.org/library/Enc/NewClassicalMacroeconomics.html. Retrieved 13 July 2010.

Howitt, Peter (2002). Snowdon, Brian; Vane, Howard. eds. *An Encyclopedia of Macroeconomics*. Cheltenham: Edward Elgar Publishing.

Kirman, Alan P. (1992). "Whom or What does the Representative Individual Represent?". *Journal of Economic Perspectives* 6 (2): 117–136.

Kocherlakota, Narayana R. (May 2010). "Modern macroeconomic models as tools for economic policy". The Region. Federal Reserve Bank of Minneapolis.

Krugman, Paul (2 September 2009). "How Did Economists Get It So Wrong?". The Concise Encyclopedia of Economics. The New York Times. http://www.nytimes.com/2009/09/06/magazine/06Economic-t.html. Retrieved 16 February 2011.

Krugman, Paul; Wells, Robin (2009). *Economics*. New York: Worth Publishers.

Kydland, Finn E.; Prescott, Edward C. (1982). "Time to Build and Aggregate Fluctuations". *Econometrica* 50 (6): 1345–1370.

Long, John B., Jr.; Plosser, Charles (1983). "Real Business Cycles". *Journal of Political Economy* 91 (1): 39–69.

Lucas, Robert E., Jr. (1977). "Understanding Business Cycles". *Carnegie-Rochester Conference Series on Public Policy* 5: 7–29.

Mankiw, N. Gregory (December 1990). "A Quick Referesher Course in Macroeconomics". *Journal of Economic Literature* 28 (4): 1645-1660.

Mark, Nelson Chung (2001). *International macroeconomics and finance: theory and econometric methods.* Oxford: Cambridge.

McCallum, Bennett T. (2008). "Monetarism". *The Concise Encyclopedia of Economics.* Library of Economics and Liberty. http://www.econlib.org/library/Enc/Monetarism.html. Retrieved 27 June 2010.

Mishkin, Frederic (2004). The Economics of Money, Banking, and Financial Markets. Boston: Pearson.

Plosser, Charles I. (1989). "Understanding real business cycles". *Journal of Economic Perspectives* 3: 51–77.

Quiggin, John (15 October 2010). "Five Zombie Economic Ideas That Refuse to Dies". Foreign Policy.

Romer, David (1993). "The New Keynesian Synthesis". *The Journal of Economic Perspectives* 7 (1): 5-22.

Sargent, Thomas J. (2008). "Rational Expectations". The Concise Encyclopedia of Economics. Library of Economics and Liberty. http://www.econlib.org/library/Enc/RationalExpectations.html. Retrieved 13 July 2010.

Skidelsky, Robert (2003). *John Maynard Keynes, 1883-1946.* New York: Penguin Books.

Snowdon, Brian and Vane, Howard R., (2005). *Modern Macroeconomics: Its Origin, Development and Current State.* Edward Elgar Publishing.

Snowdon, Brian; Howard Vane (2005). *Modern Macroeconomics.* Cheltenham: E. Elgar.

Summers, Lawrence H. (1986). "Some Skeptical Observations on Real Business Cycle Theory". *Federal Reserve Bank of Minneapolis Quarterly Review* 10 (Fall): 23–27.

Woodford, Michael (2009). "Convergence in Macroeconomics:Elements of the New Synthesis". *American Economic Journal: Macroeconomics 1* (1): 267–79.

3

Austrian Business Cycle Theory

"There is sometimes as much ability in knowing how to profit by good advice as in arriving at a correct opinion ourselves."

—*Francois De La Rochefoucauld*

In the realm of macroeconomics, the Austrian business cycle theory ("ABCT") attempts to explain business cycles through a set of ideas held by the heterodox Austrian School of economics. The theory views business cycles (or, as some Austrians prefer, "credit cycles") as the inevitable consequence of excessive growth in bank credit, exacerbated by inherently damaging and ineffective central bank policies, which cause interest rates to remain too low for too long, resulting in excessive credit creation, speculative economic bubbles and lowered savings. Proponents believe that a sustained period of low interest rates and excessive credit creation results in a volatile and unstable imbalance between saving and investment.

According to the theory, the business cycle unfolds in the following way: Low interest rates tend to stimulate borrowing from the banking system. This expansion of credit causes an expansion of the supply of money, through the money creation process in a fractional reserve banking system. It is asserted that this leads to an unsustainable credit-sourced boom during which the artificially stimulated borrowing seeks out diminishing investment opportunities. Though disputed, proponents hold that a credit-sourced boom results in widespread malinvestments. In the theory, a correction or "credit crunch" – commonly called a "recession" or "bust" – occurs when exponential credit creation cannot be sustained.

Then the money supply suddenly and sharply contracts when markets finally "clear", causing resources to be reallocated back towards more efficient uses. Given these perceived damaging and disruptive effects caused by what Austrian scholars believe to be volatile and unsustainable growth in credit-sourced money, many proponents (such as Murray Rothbard) advocate either heavy regulation of the banking system (strictly enforcing a policy of full reserves on the banks) or, more often, free banking.

The main proponents of the Austrian business cycle theory historically were Ludwig von Mises and Friedrich Hayek. Hayek won a Nobel Prize in economics in 1974 (shared with Gunnar Myrdal) in part for his work on this theory. The Austrian explanation of the business cycle varies significantly from the mainstream understanding of business cycles, and is generally rejected by mainstream economists. Economists such as Milton Friedman, Gordon Tullock, Bryan Caplan, and Paul Krugman have said that they regard the Austrian explanation as incorrect.

Further, the Austrian school's methods of deriving theories have been criticized by mainstream economists as *a priori* "non-empirical" analysis and differing from the practices of scientific theorizing, as widely conducted in economics.

It is apt to mention that trade cycle argument first appeared in the last few pages of Ludwig von Mises's *The*

Theory of Money and Credit (1912). This early development of Austrian business cycle theory was a direct manifestation of Mises's rejection of the concept of neutral money and emerged as an almost incidental by-product of his exploration of the theory of banking.

David Laidler has observed in a chapter on the theory that the origins lie in the ideas of Knut Wicksell.

Austrian economist Roger Garrison explains the origins of the theory:

> Grounded in the economic theory set out in Carl Menger's *Principles of Economics* and built on the vision of a capital-using production process developed in Eugen von Böhm-Bawerk's *Capital and Interest*, the Austrian theory of the business cycle remains sufficiently distinct to justify its national identification. But even in its earliest rendition in Ludwig von Mises' *Theory of Money and Credit* and in subsequent exposition and extension in F.A. Hayek's *Prices and Production*, the theory incorporated important elements from Swedish and British economics.
>
> Knut Wicksell's *Interest and Prices*, which showed how prices respond to a discrepancy between the bank rate and the real rate of interest, provided the basis for the Austrian account of the misallocation of capital during the boom. The market process that eventually reveals the intertemporal misallocation and turns boom into bust resembles an analogous process described by the British Currency School, in which international misallocations induced by credit expansion are subsequently eliminated by changes in the terms of trade and hence in specie flow.

Now a popularized version of the theory is presented in Murray Rothbard's pamphlet *Economic Depressions: Their Cause and Cure*, which endeavors to explain the business cycle by focusing on excessive bank-sourced credit expansion and centralized government intervention (through the actions of a central bank). Rothbard went into much greater detail in his book *What Has Government Done to Our Money?*.

Main Issues

The Austrian business cycle theory attempts to answer the following questions about things which Austrian theorists, notably Murray Rothbard, believe appear during the business cycle:

- Why is there a sudden general cluster of business errors?
- Why do capital goods industries and asset market prices fluctuate more widely than do the consumer goods industries and consumer prices?
- Why is there a general increase in the quantity of money in the economy during every boom, and why is there generally, though not universally, a fall in the money supply during the depression (or a sharp contraction in the growth of credit in a recession)?

According to the theory, the boom-bust cycle of malinvestment is generated by excessive and unsustainable credit expansion to businesses and individual borrowers by the banks. This credit creation makes it appear as if the supply of "saved funds" ready for investment has increased, for the effect is the same: the supply of funds for investment purposes increases, and the interest rate is lowered. Borrowers, in short, are misled by the bank inflation into believing that the supply of saved funds (the pool of "deferred" funds ready to be invested) is greater than it really is.

When the pool of "saved funds" increases, entrepreneurs invest in "longer process of production," i.e., the capital structure is lengthened, especially in the "higher orders", most remote from the consumer. Borrowers take their newly acquired funds and bid up the prices of capital and other producers' goods, which, in the theory, stimulates a shift of investment from consumer goods to capital goods industries. Austrians further contend that such a shift is unsustainable and must reverse itself in due course.

Despite mainstream findings of evidence to the contrary, proponents of the theory conclude that the longer the unsustainable shift in capital goods industries continues, the more violent and disruptive the necessary re-adjustment process. While agreeing with economist Tyler Cowen, Bryan Caplan has stated that he also denies "that the artificially stimulated investments have any tendency to become malinvestments." The preference by entrepreneurs for longer term investments can be shown graphically by using any discounted cash flow model. Essentially lower interest rates increase the relative value of cash flows that come in the future.

When modelling an investment opportunity, if interest rates are artificially low, entrepreneurs are led to believe the income they will receive in the future is sufficient to cover their near term investment costs. In simple terms, investments that would not make sense with a 10% cost of funds become feasible with a prevailing interest rate of 5% (and may become compelling for many entrepreneurs with a prevailing interest rate of 2%). The proportion of consumption to saving or investment is determined by people's time preferences, which is the degree to which they prefer present to future satisfactions.

Thus, the pure interest rate is determined by the time preferences of the individuals in society, and the final market rates of interest reflect the pure interest rate plus or minus the entrepreneurial risk and purchasing power components. Because the debasement of the means of exchange is universal, many entrepreneurs can make the same mistake at the same time (i.e. many believe investment funds are really available for long term projects when in fact the pool of available funds has come from credit creation - not real savings out of the existing money supply).

As they are all competing for the same pool of capital and market share, some entrepreneurs begin to borrow simply to avoid being "overrun" by other entrepreneurs who may take advantage of the lower interest rates to invest in more up-to-date capital infrastructure. A tendency towards over-investment and speculative borrowing in this "artificial" low interest rate environment is therefore almost inevitable. This new money then percolates downward from the business borrowers to the factors of production: to the landowners and capital owners who sold assets to the newly indebted entrepreneurs, and then to the other factors of production in wages, rent, and interest.

Austrian economists conclude that, since time preferences have not changed, people will rush to reestablish the old proportions, and demand will shift back from the higher to the lower orders. In other words, depositors will tend to remove cash from the banking system and spend it (not save it), banks will then ask their borrowers for payment and interest rates and credit conditions will deteriorate.

It is pertinent to note that Austrian economists theorize that capital goods industries will find that their investments have been in error; that what they thought profitable really fails for lack of demand by their entrepreneurial customers. Higher orders of production will have turned out to be wasteful, and the malinvestment must be liquidated. In other words, the particular *types* of investments made during the monetary boom were inappropriate and "wrong" from the perspective of the long-term financial sustainability of the market because the price signals stimulating the investment were distorted by fractional reserve banking's recursive lending "ballooning" the pricing structure in various capital markets. This concept is captured by the term "heterogeneity of capital", where Austrian economists emphasize that the mere macroeconomic "total" of investment does not adequately capture whether this investment is genuinely sustainable or productive, due to the inability of the raw numbers to reveal the particular investment activities being undertaken and the inherent inability of the numbers to reveal whether these particular investment activities were appropriate and economically sustainable given people's real preferences. Though disputed, Austrian scholars assert that the boom then, is actually a period of wasteful malinvestment, a "false boom" where the particular kinds of investments undertaken during the period of fiat money expansion are revealed to lead nowhere but to insolvency and unsustainability.

It is the time when errors are made, when speculative borrowing has driven up prices for assets and capital to unsustainable levels, due to low interest rates "artificially" increasing the money supply and triggering an unsustainable injection of fiat money "funds" available for investment into the system, thereby tampering with the complex pricing mechanism of the free market. "Real" savings would have required higher interest rates to encourage depositors to save their money in term deposits to invest in longer term projects under a stable money supply.

According to von Mises's work, the artificial stimulus caused by bank-created credit causes a generalized speculative investment bubble, not justified by the long-term structure of the market. Ludwig von Mises further suggests that a "crisis" (or "credit crunch") arrives when the consumers come to reestablish their desired allocation of saving and consumption at prevailing interest rates. The "recession" or "depression" is actually the process by which the economy adjusts to the wastes and errors of the monetary boom, and reestablishes efficient service of sustainable consumer desires.

It is pertinent to note that since it takes very little time for the new credit-sourced money to filter down from the initial borrowers to the recipients of the borrowed funds (the various factors of production), why don't all booms come quickly to an end? Austrians assert that continually expanding bank credit can keep the borrowers one step ahead of consumer retribution (with the help of successively lower interest rates from the central bank). In the theory, this postpones the "day of reckoning" and defers the collapse of unsustainably inflated asset prices.

It can also be temporarily put off by price deflation or exogenous events such as the "cheap" or free acquisition of marketable resources by market participants and the banks funding the borrowing (such as the acquisition of land from local governments, or in extreme cases, the acquisition of foreign land through the waging of war). Austrian scholars theorize that the monetary boom ends when bank credit expansion finally stops - when no further investments can be found which provide adequate returns for speculative borrowers at prevailing interest rates.

It is asserted that the longer the "false" monetary boom goes on, the bigger and more speculative the borrowing, the more wasteful the errors committed and the longer and more severe will be the necessary bankruptcies, foreclosures and depression readjustment., though Milton Friedman concluded that the Austrian claim contradicts the evidence examined in his studies. There is also a notion of capital consumption contributing negatively to the readjustment period, which has been discussed in works such as *Human Action*.

It is pertinent to note that Ludwig von Mises and Friedrich Hayek warned of a major economic crisis before the Great Depression. Hayek made his prediction of a coming business crisis in February 1929. He warned that a financial crisis was an unavoidable consequence of reckless monetary expansion.

The Role of Central Banks

In fact, all Austrian theorists consider the unsustainable expansion of bank credit through fractional reserve banking as the driving feature of most business cycles. However, Murray Rothbard paid particular attention to the role of central banks in creating an environment of loose credit prior to the onset of the Great Depression, and the subsequent ineffectiveness of central bank policies, which simply delayed necessary price adjustments and prolonged market dysfunction.

Rothbard begins with the claim that in a market with no centralized monetary authority, there would be no simultaneous cluster of malinvestments or entrepreneurial errors, since astute entrepreneurs would not all make errors at the same time and would quickly take advantage of any temporary, isolated mispricing. In addition, in an open, non-centralized (uninsured) capital market, astute bankers would shy away from speculative lending and uninsured depositors would carefully monitor the balance sheets of risky financial institutions, tempering any speculative excesses that arose sporadically in the finance markets. In Rothbard's view, the cycle of *generalized* malinvestment is greatly exacerbated by *centralized* monetary intervention in the money markets by the central bank.

Such propositions from Rothbard prompted criticism from Bryan Caplan, who questions "Why does Rothbard think businessmen are so incompetent at forecasting government policy? He credits them with entrepreneurial foresight about all market-generated conditions, but curiously finds them unable to forecast government policy, or even to avoid falling prey to simple accounting illusions generated by inflation and deflation... Particularly in interventionist economies, it would seem that natural selection would weed out businesspeople with such a gigantic blind spot."

However, Rothbard asserts that an over-encouragement to borrow and lend is initiated by the mispricing of credit via the central bank's *centralized* control over interest rates and its need to protect banks from periodic bank runs (which Austrian economists believe then causes interest rates to be set too low for too long when compared to the rates that would prevail in a genuine non-central bank dominated free market). Under the current fiat monetary system, a central bank creates new money when it lends to member banks, and this money is multiplied many times over through the money creation process of the private banks. This new bank-created money enters the loan market and provides a lower rate of interest than that which would prevail if the money supply were stable.

An Analysis of Financial Crisis (2007–2010)

In fact, the financial crisis of 2007-2010 has resulted in a revival of interest in the Austrian business cycle theory, but has also resulted in a revival of interest of theories more critical of Austrian theory, such as Keynesianism and Post-Keynesian economics. After the United States housing bubble began its decline in 2006, Peter Schiff, a supporter of the Austrian school, made some predictions regarding a housing crash in the US, though (as of early 2009) Schiff's investment firm had not been able to profit from strategies based on his predictions. Ron Paul also spoke about the Austrian business cycle repeatedly throughout his 2008 presidential campaign.

Other Theories

The Austrian theory is considered one of the precursors to the modern credit cycle theory, which is emphasized by Post-Keynesian economists, economists at the Bank for International Settlements, and by a few mainstream academics such as Hyman Minsky and Charles P. Kindleberger. These two emphasize asymmetric information and agency problems. (Henry George, another precursor, emphasized the negative impact of speculative increases in the value of land, which places a heavy burden of mortgage payments on consumers and companies.) A different theory of credit cycles is the debt-deflation theory of Irving Fisher, which is today placed in the Post-Keynesian tradition.

The difference between these may be stated as debt-deflation being a *demand*-side theory, which emphasizes the period *after* the peak – the end of a credit bubble and contraction of debt causing a fall in *aggregate demand* – while the Austrian theory is a *supply*-side theory, which emphasizes the period *before* the peak – the growth of debt during the growth phase causing malinvestment.

The theories may thus be seen as complementary, addressing different aspects of the issue, and are so-considered by some economists. In 2003 Barry Eichengreen laid out modern credit boom theory as a cycle in which loans increase as the economy expands, particularly where regulation is weak, and through these loans money supply increases. Inflation remains low, however, because of either a pegged exchange rate or a supply shock, and thus the central bank does not tighten credit and money.

Increasingly speculative loans are made as diminishing returns lead to reduced yields. Eventually inflation begins or the economy slows, and when asset prices decline, a bubble is pricked which encourages a macroeconomic bust.

It is significant to note that 2006 William White argued that "financial liberalization has increased the likelihood of boom-bust cycles of the Austrian sort". While White conceded that the status quo policy had been successful in reducing the impacts of busts, he commented that the view on inflation should perhaps be longer term and that the excesses of the time seemed dangerous.

In addition, White believes that the Austrian explanation of the business cycle might be relevant once again in an environment of excessively low interest rates. According to the theory, a sustained period of low interest rates and excessive credit creation results in a volatile and unstable imbalance between saving and investment.

In 1969, Milton Friedman, after examining the history of business cycles in the US, concluded that "The Hayek-Mises explanation of the business cycle is contradicted by the evidence. It is, I believe, false." He analyzed the issue using newer data in 1993, and again reached the same conclusions. In 2001, Austrian economist James P. Keeler stated that the hypotheses of the theory are consistent with his preliminary empirical research.

Critical Analysis

In fact, the Austrian theory of the business cycle is now rarely discussed by mainstream economists, but was more actively debated in the mid-20th century. Nobel laureate Hayek's formulation of the theory in the 1930s was harshly criticized by John Maynard Keynes, Piero Sraffa and Nicholas Kaldor. In 1932, Piero Sraffa argued that Hayek's formulation of the business cycle required a kind of money that was entirely neutral, and was in effect a simple commodity, unable to act as a store of value or be loaned at interest.

Hayek reformulated his theory in response to those objections, but his reformulation was then criticised by Nicholas Kaldor in 1939 and again in 1942. More recently, mainstream economists like Nobel laureate Milton Friedman, Gordon Tullock, Bryan Caplan, and Paul Krugman have stated that they regard the theory as incorrect.

David Laidler views the theory as motivated by the political leanings of its major proponents, as Austrian economists are known for their strong opposition to government involvement in the economy, and argues that the theory was discredited because of its association with "nihilistic policy prescriptions" for the Great Depression. On the other hand, Laidler also stated that its core insights were materially worthwhile, especially as related to the work of Dennis Robertson. In 1988 Gordon Tullock explained his disagreement with the theory. His main point is that "if the process that Rothbard describes did occur, there would be many corporate bankruptcies and business people jumping out of the windows of office buildings, but there would be only minor transitional unemployment. In fact, measured GNP would be higher as a result."

This is because the Austrian theory implies fluctuations in investment, but not in the production decisions of firms. Paul Krugman also made a similar argument when he stated that the theory implies that consumption would increase during downturns and cannot explain the empirical observation that spending in *all sectors* of the economy falls during a recession.

It is apt to mention that mainstream economists argue

that the theory requires bankers and investors to exhibit a kind of irrationality – that they be regularly fooled into making unprofitable investments by temporarily low interest rates. Critics have also argued that, as the theory points to the actions of fractional-reserve banks and central banks to explain business cycles, it fails to explain the existence of business cycles before the establishment of Federal Reserve in 1913. For example, the Panic of 1873 would initiate the Long Depression in US and much of Europe. Additionally, there were also severe market crashes in the United States of the magnitude of the 1929 crash in 1869, 1882, 1884, 1896, 1901, and 1907; there was no central bank or national monetary policy in the US during these crises.

In fact, the movement to establish central banking in the United States was in part a response to the business cycle, particularly the Panic of 1907. Mainstream economists believe that economies have experienced less severe boom-bust cycles after World War II, since central banks have started using monetary policy to stabilize economies – see especially The Great Moderation.

With regards to the criticism which concludes that the Austrian Business Cycle theory requires widespread irrationality about the future of interest rates, Austrian thinkers Carilli and Dempster have offered a response. They have argued that a prisoner's dilemma framework can explain the apparent failure of investors to learn from previous experience. In response to several severe economic crashes that occurred without a central bank, historian Thomas Woods argues in his book *Meltdown* that the crashes were caused by various privately-owned banks (with state charters) which issued paper money, supposedly convertible to gold, in amounts greatly exceeding their gold reserves.

After having a view of Austrian Business cycle theory, in the next chapter we will discuss supply-side economics.

REFERENCES

Block W, Barnett II W. (2007). On Laidler regarding the Austrian business cycle theory. *Review of Austrian Economics.*

Caplan, Bryan (2008-01-02). "What's Wrong With Austrian Business Cycle Theory". Library of Economics and Liberty.

Friedman, Milton. "The 'Plucking Model' of Business Fluctuations Revisited". *Economic Inquiry*: 171–177.

Friedman, Milton. "The Monetary Studies of the National Bureau, 44th Annual Report". *The Optimal Quantity of Money and Other Essays*. Chicago: Aldine. pp. 261–284.

Garrison, Roger. In *Business Cycles and Depressions*. David Glasner, ed. New York: Garland Publishing Co., 1997, pp. 23-27.

Gordon, Tullock (1988). "Why the Austrians are wrong about depressions" (PDF). *The Review of Austrian Economics* 2 (1): 73–78.

Keeler, JP. (2001). Empirical Evidence on the Austrian Business Cycle Theory. *Review of Austrian Economics* 14 (4).

Krugman, Paul (1998-12-04). "The Hangover Theory". Slate. http://www.slate.com/id/9593. Retrieved 2008-06-20.

Laider, D. (1999). *Fabricating the Keynesian Revolution*. Cambridge University Press. Preview.

Mayer, Thomas (Winter 1998). "Boettke's Austrian critique of mainstream economics: An empiricist's response". *Critical Review* (Routledge): 151–171.

Pierro Sraffa (1932). "Dr. Hayek on Money and Capital". *Economic Journal (reprinted in Hayek 1995)* 42 (March): 42–53.

Samuelson, Paul A. (Sep 1964). "Theory and Realism: A Reply". *The American Economic Review* (American Economic Association): 736–739.

White, Lawrence H. (2008), "The research program of Austrian economics", *Advances in Austrian Economics* (Emerald Group Publishing Limited): 20

White, William (April 2006) (PDF). *Is Price Stability Enough?*. Bank for International Settlements.

Woods, Jr., Thomas (2007). "22:Did Capitalism Cause the Great Depression?". *33 Questions about American History You're Not Supposed to Ask*. New York: Crown Forum. pp. 174–179.

4

Supply-Side Economics

> "Remember that there is nothing stable in human affairs; therefore avoid undue elation in prosperity, or undue depression in adversity."
>
> —*Socrates*

It is apt to mention first that supply-side economics is a school of macroeconomic thought that argues that economic growth can be most effectively created by lowering barriers for people to produce (supply) goods and services, such as adjusting income tax and capital gains tax rates, and by allowing greater flexibility by reducing regulation.

According to the theory, consumers will then benefit from a greater supply of goods and services at lower prices.

Remarkably, current supply-side economics is primarily concerned with economic growth in general, and does not hold that decreasing taxes increases government revenue. It is true that many early proponents argued that the size of the economic growth would be significant enough that the increased government revenue from a faster growing economy would be sufficient to compensate completely for the short-term costs of a tax cut, and that tax cuts could, in fact, cause overall revenue to increase. However, in 2003, the Wall Street Journal declared the debate over the ability of supply-side economics to reduce taxes without cost has ended "with a whimper," after extensive modeling performed by the Congressional Budget Office (CBO) failed to support that possibility.

Basically, the term "supply-side economics" was thought, for some time, to have been coined by journalist Jude Wanniski in 1975, but according to Robert D. Atkinson's *Supply-Side Follies* [p. 50], the term "supply side" ("supply-side fiscalists") was first used by Herbert Stein, a former economic adviser to President Nixon, in 1976, and only later that year was this term repeated by Jude Wanniski. Its use connotes the ideas of economists Robert Mundell and Arthur Laffer. Today, supply-side economics is often conflated with the politically rhetorical term "trickle-down economics", but as Jude Wanniski points out in his book *The Way The World Works*, trickle-down economics is conservative Keynesianism associated with the Democratic Party's views of the Republican Party platform. Typical policy recommendations of supply-side economics are lower marginal tax rates and less regulation.

Maximum benefits from taxation policy are achieved by optimizing the marginal tax rates to spur growth, although it is a common misunderstanding that supply side economics is concerned only with taxation policy when it is about removing barriers to production more generally.

Now we will discuss the historical origin of this theory.

In fact, supply-side economics developed during the 1970s in response to Keynesian economic policy, and in particular the failure of demand management to stabilize Western economies during the stagflation of the 1970s, in the wake of the oil crisis in 1973. It drew on a range of non-Keynesian economic thought, particularly Austrian school thinking on entrepreneurship and new classical macroeconomics.

The intellectual roots of supply-side economics have also been traced back to various early economic thinkers such as Ibn Khaldun, Jonathan Swift, David Hume, Adam Smith and Alexander Hamilton. As in classical economics, supply-side economics proposed that production or supply is the key to economic prosperity and that consumption or demand is merely a secondary consequence.

Early on this idea had been summarized in Say's Law of economics, which states: "A product is no sooner created, than it, from that instant, affords a market for other products to the full extent of its own value." John Maynard Keynes, the founder of Keynesianism, summarized Say's Law as "supply creates its own demand." He turned Say's Law on its head in the 1930s by declaring that demand creates its own supply. However, Say's Law does not state that production creates a demand for the product itself, but rather a demand for "*other products to the full extent of its own value.*"

A better formulation of the law is that the supply of one good constitutes demand for one or more other goods. This requires that the original good has some value to another party and it is through willingness to trade this value that the producer of the new good can express his demand for another good. In 1978, Jude Wanniski published *The Way the World Works*, in which he laid out the central thesis of supply-side economics and detailed the failure of high tax-rate progressive income tax systems and U.S. monetary policy under Nixon in the 1970s. Wanniski advocated lower tax rates and a return to some kind of gold standard, similar to the 1944-1971 Bretton Woods System that Nixon abandoned.

Victor Canto, a disciple of Arthur Laffer, published *The Foundations of Supply-Side Economics* in 1983. This theory focuses on the effects of marginal tax rates on the incentive to work and save, which affect the growth of the "supply side" or what Keynesians call potential output. While the latter focus on changes in the rate of supply-side growth in the long run, the "new" supply-siders often promised short-term results.

In fact, the supply-siders were influenced strongly by the idea of the Laffer curve, which states that tax *rates* and tax *revenues* were distinct—that tax rates too high or too low will not maximize tax revenues. Supply-siders felt that in a high tax rate environment, lowering taxes to the right level can raise revenue by causing faster economic growth.

They pointed to the tax cuts of the Kennedy administration and the high rates of the Hoover and Nixon administrations in justification. This led the supply-siders to advocate large reductions in marginal income and capital gains tax rates to encourage allocation of assets to investment, which would produce more supply. Jude Wanniski and many others advocate a zero capital gains rate.

The increased aggregate supply would result in increased aggregate demand, hence the term "Supply-Side Economics". Furthermore, in response to inflation, supply-siders called for indexed marginal income tax rates, as monetary inflation had pushed wage earners into higher marginal income tax brackets that remained static; that is, as wages increased to maintain purchasing power with prices, income tax brackets were not adjusted accordingly and thus wage earners were pushed into higher income tax brackets than tax policy had intended.

It is notable that supply-side economics has been criticized as essentially politically conservative. Supply-side advocates claim that they are not following an ideology, but are reinstating classical economics. Yet, supply-siders such as Jude Wanniski have argued for lower tax rates to increase tax revenues, and that redistribution of income through taxation was essential to the health of the polity — a view that is anathema to traditional conservatives. Some economists see similarities between supply-side proposals and Keynesian economics. If the result of changes to the tax structure is a fiscal deficit then the 'supply-side' policy is effectively stimulating demand through the Keynesian multiplier effect.

Supply-side proponents would point out, in response, that the level of taxation and spending is important for economic incentives, not just the size of the deficit. The Reagan administration justified such changes in socioeconomic terms by invoking the old saying that "a rising tide lifts all boats".

Both supply-siders and their opponents have been keen to claim the mantles of thinkers as diverse as Karl Marx and Adam Smith. Jude Wanniski has claimed both as supply-side thinkers due to their advocacy of a gold monetary standard and more specifically their focus on the agents of production in an economy. Barton Biggs, chief investment strategist of Morgan Stanley, described Wanniski's book about supply-side economics, *The Way the World Works*, as the "most important" economic book published since Marx's writings.

Fiscal Policy Theory

Supply-side economics holds that increased taxation steadily reduces economic trade between economic participants within a nation and that it discourages investment. Taxes act as a type of trade barrier or tariff that causes economic participants to revert to less efficient means of satisfying their needs. As such, higher taxation leads to lower levels of specialization and lower economic efficiency. The idea is said to be illustrated by the Laffer curve. (Case & Fair, 1999: 780, 781). Crucial to the operation of supply-side theory is the expansion of free trade and free movement of capital. It is argued that free capital movement, in addition to the classical reasoning of comparative advantage, frequently allows an economic expansion.

Lowering tax barriers to trade provides to the domestic economy all the advantages that the international economy gets from lower tariff barriers.

Basically, supply-side economists have less to say on the effects of deficits, and sometimes cite Robert Barro's work that states that rational economic actors will buy bonds in sufficient quantities to reduce long term interest rates. Critics argue that standard exchange rate theory would predict, instead, a devaluation of the currency of the nation running the high budget deficit, and eventual "crowding out" of private investment.

It is apt here to quote Mundell who say, "Fiscal discipline is a learned behavior." To put it another way, eventually the unfavourable effects of running persistent budget deficits will force governments to reduce spending in line with their levels of revenue. This view is also promoted by Victor Canto. The central issue at stake is the point of diminishing returns on liquidity in the investment sector: Is there a point where additional money is "pushing on a string"? To the supply-side economist, reallocation away from consumption to private investment, and most especially from public investment to private investment, will always yield superior economic results.

In standard monetarist and Keynesian theory, however, there will be a point where increases in asset prices will produce no new supply. A point where investment demand outruns potential investment supply, and produce instead asset inflation, or in common terms a bubble. The existence of this point, and where it is should it exist, is the essential question of the efficacy of supply-side economics.

Monetary Policy Theory

Some supply-siders advocate that monetary policy should be based on a price rule. The aim of monetary policy should be to target a specific value of money irrespective of the quantity of money that must be created or withdrawn by the central bank to achieve this target. This contrasts with monetarism's focus on the quantity of money, and Keynesian theory's emphasis on real aggregate demand.

The important difference is that to a monetarist the quantity of money, specifically represented by the money supply is the crucial determining variable for the relationship between the supply and demand for money, while to a Keynesian adequate demand to support the available money supply is important. Keynes famously remarked that "money doesn't matter". This is an area where supply-side theory has been particularly influential. Under macroeconomic theory, the general level of price was based on the strict increase in price of a basket of goods. Under supply-side theory, the rate of inflation should be based on the substitutions that individuals make in the market place, and should take into account the improved quality of goods.

In the late 1980s and through the 1990s, under Presidents of both American political parties, shifts were made in the calculation of the broadly followed measure of inflation the "Consumer Price Index for Urban Consumers", or CPI-W, which reflected supply-side ideas on substitution. The argument for factoring in goods' quality was not accepted, which has led supply-side economists to claim that the actual CPI is actually between 0.5% and 1% lower than the stated rate.

Basically, this area represents one of the points of contention between conservative economic theorists who argue for a quantity of money theory of inflation, including Austrian economics, many strict gold standard economists and traditional monetarists, and supply-side theorists.

According to the increases in money supply during the 1990s, the real rate of inflation must be higher than is currently stated. These economists argue that the cost of housing is understated in the CPI-W, and that the inflation rate should be between 0.5% and 1% higher. It is for this reason that many central bankers, investment analysts and economists follow the GDP deflator which measures the total output of the society and the prices paid for all goods, not merely consumer goods. Some supply-siders view gold as the best unit of account with which to measure the price of fiat money, which is defined as a money supply not directly limited by specie or hard assets.

Hence the purest supply-siders are in general advocates of a gold standard. However the reverse is not true; many gold standard advocates are harsh critics of supply-side economics. Supply-side economists assert that the value of money is purely dictated by the supply and demand for money. In fiat money system the government has a legislated monopoly on the supply of base money. Hence it has some control over the value of money. Any decline in the value of money (or appreciation) is then viewed by some as the result of errant central bank policy.

Tax Revenues

Notably, many early proponents argued that the size of the economic growth would be significant enough that the increased government revenue from a faster growing economy would be sufficient to compensate completely for the short-term costs of a tax cut, and that tax cuts could, in fact, cause overall revenue to increase.

Some hold this was borne out during the 1980s when, advocates of supply-side economics claim, tax cuts ultimately led to an overall increase in governmental revenue due to stronger economic growth. Other economists, however, dispute this assertion. Some contemporary economists do not consider supply-side economics a tenable economic theory, with Alan Blinder calling it an "ill-fated" and perhaps "silly" school on the pages of a 2006 textbook. Greg Mankiw, former chairman of President George W. Bush's Council of Economic Advisors, offered similarly sharp criticism of the school in the early editions of his introductory economics textbook.

In a 1992 article for the *Harvard International Review,* James Tobin wrote, "[The] idea that tax cuts would actually increase revenues turned out to deserve the ridicule..." While few modern economists claim that tax cuts will completely pay for themselves, some empirical and theoretical research suggests that tax cuts do help to pay for themselves through increased economic growth, though the end result, even conservative economists contend, will be a significant reduction in revenues. The Reagan administration was the first to implement supply-side policies and call them that.

Some maintain that they failed to deliver the promised benefits.

> The extreme promises of supply-side economics did not materialize. President Reagan argued that because of the effect depicted in the Laffer curve, the government could maintain expenditures, cut tax rates, *and* balance the

> budget. This was not the case. Government revenues fell sharply from levels that would have been realized without the tax cuts.
>
> - *Karl Case & Ray Fair, Principles of Economics (2007), p. 695.*

Remarkably, supply side proponents Trabandt and Uhlig argue that "static scoring overestimates the revenue loss for labor and capital tax cuts", and that instead "dynamic scoring" is a better predictor for the effects of tax cuts.

It should be noted, however, that many supply side economists do not view the decrease in governmental revenue as problematic. Rather, they believe that the associated increases in real investment and standard of living more than make up for reduced government spending.

U.S. Monetary and Fiscal Experience: An Example

Supply-side economists seek a cause and effect relationship between lowering marginal rates on capital formation and economic expansion. The supply-side history of economics since the 1960s hinges on the following key turning points:

In 1971, Richard Nixon ended the convertibility of the US dollar into gold, which meant the end of the Bretton Woods system. Commodity prices, including oil and gold particularly, which had been rising steadily in response to the dollar glut, spiked upwards. The supply-side explanation for this event is that taxation on investment had depleted the incentive to capital investment either in new sources of materials or in substitute goods, which when combined with eroding confidence in the U.S. dollar cause it to be rapidly devalued.

Many supply siders agree with gold investors in saying that the value of commodities remained constant and that it was the dollar that devalued. At the same time the Mundell-Fleming model of currency flows gained greater credence when it was codified into a single set of equations, and became increasingly influential in neo-liberal economics.

The argument for a floating currency regime had first been adopted by Friedman, but supply-side economists such as Wanniski typically argued that exchange rates should be fixed relative to gold. Mundell was the author of the influential view that it was Johnson's budget deficits that were the cause of inflationary pressure. However, as Lester Thurow pointed out, the standard model of inflationary pressure shows that Johnson's peak year of deficits would have created only a small upward pressure, that instead it was persistent American trade deficits through the 1960s which had a greater effect on the imbalance between the value of the U.S. dollar and the gold to which it was, in theory, convertible.

Stagflation

Basically, stagflation is defined as a period of slow economic growth and high unemployment (stagnation) while prices rise (inflation). Robert Mundell believes Nixon's failure to cut taxes in the early 1970s to be the cause of stagflation, his argument being that the incentive for individuals to invest was reduced to below zero. Measuring the S&P 500 in inflation-adjusted terms, the stock market lost half of its value between the market peak of 1972 and its bottom in 1982, with money seeking better returns in real estate and commodities instead. The argument from the supply-side point of view then goes on to state that the cuts in capital gains tax rates that were part of the 1981 tax package returned incentives to invest.

The Keynesian point of view is that after a long bear market, money had fled from stocks and was set to return, once the expectation of inflation had been reduced. Neither of these two arguments fully accounts for the rise of equities over the course of the "long Bull Market" of 1982-2000.

As such the importance of this argument needs to be seen in light of the effects of the inflation of the late 1970s, where credit became constricted, as interest rates rose rapidly, and the number of borrowers who could qualify for even standard mortgages fell. Inflation acted as a tax on wage increases, because the highly progressive income tax system of the time meant that more and more households suffered from "bracket creep" - in which a wage increase would be reduced in value by the increased taxes collected. The effects of inflation produced, in 1980, a strong political consensus for a change in basic policy.

Reaganomics

U.S. President Ronald Reagan made supply-side economics a household phrase, and promised an across the board reduction in income tax rates and an even larger reduction in capital gains tax rates. (Case & Fair, 1999: 781, 782). When vying for the Republican party presidential nomination for the 1980 election, George H.W. Bush derided Reagan's supply-side policies as "voodoo economics". However, later he seemed to give lip service to these policies to secure the Republican nomination in 1988, and is speculated by some to have lost in his re-election bid in 1992 by allowing tax increases. The centerpiece of the supply-side argument is the economic rebound from the 1980-1982 "double-dip recession", combined with the continued fall in commodity prices. The "across the board" tax cuts of 1981 are seen as the great motivator for the "Seven Fat Years".

Critics of this view point out that the "rebound" from the recession of 1981-1982 is exactly in accordance with the "disinflation" scenario predicted by IS/LM models of the late 1970s: essentially that the increases in fed funds rates squeezed out inflation, and that federal budget deficits acted to "prime the pump". This model had been the basis of Volcker's federal reserve policy. In 1981, Robert Mundell told Ronald Reagan that by cutting upper bracket taxation rates and lowering tax rates on capital gains, national output would increase so much that tax revenues would also increase. Mundell claimed that the economic expansion would also mop up excess liquidity and bring inflation back under control.

After the tax cuts were implemented, nominal revenues quickly returned to—and ultimately surpassed—previous levels. While revenues dropped as a share of GDP, supply-siders note they intended for this fall to happen, since cutting tax rates would preclude a rise in taxes collected relative to national income. The question of whether the tax cuts proved Mundell's predictions correct has sparked much debate between supply-siders and mainstream economists. While nominal revenues rebounded after the tax cuts, mainstream economists note that comparing nominal tax collections over time fails to take into account inflation. By converting tax revenues from nominal to real terms, these economists have shown that tax revenues did not surpass their 1981 levels until 1987. Defenders of supply-side economics also complain that the focus of the debate on government revenue tends to ignore the societal benefits of economic growth, primarily lower levels of unemployment, higher wages for workers and lower prices for consumers.

This is a rhetorical argument derisively known as trickle-down economics, and should be viewed as distinct from the economic theory of supply-side economics. In the United States, commentators frequently equate supply-side economics with Reaganomics. The fiscal policies of Ronald Reagan were largely based on supply-side economics. During Reagan's 1980 presidential campaign, the key economic concern was double digit inflation, which Reagan described as "Too many dollars chasing too few goods", but rather than the usual dose of tight money, recession and layoffs, with their consequent loss of production and wealth, he promised a gradual and painless way to fight inflation by "producing our way out of it".

Switching from an earlier monetarist policy, Federal Reserve chair Paul Volcker began a policy of tighter monetary policies such as lower money supply growth to break the inflationary psychology and squeeze inflationary expectations out of the economic system. Therefore, supply-side supporters argue, "Reaganomics" was only partially based on supply-side economics. However, under Reagan, Congress passed a plan that would slash taxes by $749 billion over five years. As a result, Jason Hymowitz cited Reagan—along with Jack Kemp—as a great advocate for supply-side economics in politics and repeatedly praised his leadership. Critics of "Reaganomics" claim it failed to produce much of the exaggerated gains some supply-siders had promised. Krugman later summarized the situation: "When Ronald Reagan was elected, the supply-siders got a chance to try out their ideas. Unfortunately, they failed." Although he credited supply-side economics for being more successful than monetarism which he claimed "left the economy in ruins", he stated that supply-side economics produced results which fell "so far short of what it promised," describing the supply-side theory as "free lunches".

Krugman and other critics point to increased budget deficits during the Reagan administration as proof that the Laffer Curve is wrong. Supply-side advocates claim that revenues increased, but that spending increased faster.

However, they typically point to total revenues even though it was only income taxes rates that were cut while other taxes, notably payroll taxes were raised. That table also does not account for inflation. For example, of the increase from $600.6 billion in 1983 to $666.5 billion in 1984, $26 billion is due to inflation, $18.3 billion to corporate taxes and $21.4 billion to social insurance revenues (mostly FICA taxes). Income tax revenues in constant dollars decreased by $2.77 billion in that year. Supply-siders cannot legitimately take credit for increased FICA tax revenue, because in 1983 FICA tax rates were increased from 6.7% to 7% and the ceiling was raised by $2,100. For the self employed, the FICA tax rate went from 9.35% to 14%. The FICA tax rate increased throughout Reagan's term, jumping to 7.51% in 1988 and the ceiling was raised by 61% through Reagan's two terms. Those tax hikes on wage earners, along with inflation, are the source of the revenue gains of the early 1980s.

In fact, it has been contended by some supply-side critics that the argument to lower taxes to increase revenues was a smokescreen for "starving" the government of revenues, in the hope that the tax cuts would lead to a commensurate drop in government spending. However, this did not turn out to be the case on the spending side; Paul Samuelson called this notion "the tape worm theory—the idea that the way to get rid of a tape worm is [to] stab your patient in the stomach".

Remarkably, Reagan himself gave credence to Samuelson's argument when he used this analogy, "We can lecture our children about extravagance until we run out of voice and breath. Or we can cure their extravagance by simply reducing their allowance." There was a second smokescreen as well, closely related to the first. If there was not a drop in total government spending, what Reagan did achieve was to not only move the national debate to the right of center but to move the center itself. So, for his eight years and most of the period since then, political battles have been fought on the conservatives' turf. How much or how little to cut Federal programs became the issue du jour.

Efforts to prevent draconian cuts in discretionary programs for the poor, such as a campaign in the early 1980s by mainline Protestant denominations under the banner, "The Poor Have Suffered Enough," quickly discovered this. To this day, subsequent similar attempts to increase or restore funds for these programs only confirmed the political lesson these church bodies learned, that the repositioning of where the battle would be joined may have been Reagan's greatest domestic achievement.

Supply-side advocates like Wanniski counter that social and fiscal conservatives who supported the supply-side prescription on tax policy for this reason were misguided and did not understand the Laffer Curve. There is frequent confusion on the meaning of the term 'supply-side economics', between the related ideas of the existence of the Laffer Curve and the belief that decreasing tax rates can increase tax revenues. But many supply-side economists doubt the latter claim, while still supporting the general policy of tax cuts.

Gregory Mankiw used the term *"fad economics"* to describe the notion of tax rate cuts increasing revenue in the third edition of his Principles of Macroeconomics textbook in a section entitled "Charlatans and Cranks":

> "An example of fad economics occurred in 1980, when a small group of economists advised Presidential candidate, Ronald Reagan, that an across-the-board cut in income tax rates would raise tax revenue. They argued that if people could keep a higher fraction of their income, people

> would work harder to earn more income. Even though tax rates would be lower, income would rise by so much, they claimed, that tax revenues would rise. Almost all professional economists, including most of those who supported Reagan's proposal to cut taxes, viewed this outcome as far too optimistic. Lower tax rates might encourage people to work harder and this extra effort would offset the direct effects of lower tax rates to some extent, but there was no credible evidence that work effort would rise by enough to cause tax revenues to rise in the face of lower tax rates. ... People on fad diets put their health at risk but rarely achieve the permanent weight loss they desire. Similarly, when politicians rely on the advice of charlatans and cranks, they rarely get the desirable results they anticipate. After Reagan's election, Congress passed the cut in tax rates that Reagan advocated, but the tax cut did not cause tax revenues to rise."

A Critical Evaluation

It is pertinent to note that some economists view supply-side as an ill-conceived economic theory. Critics of supply-side economics point to the lack of academic economics credentials by movement leaders such as Jude Wanniski and Robert Bartley to imply that the theories behind it are bankrupt. David Harper and others dismiss the theory as offering "nothing particularly new or controversial" to an updated view of classical economics. Paul Krugman published a book dedicated to attacking the theory, and Reaganomics, under the title "Peddling Prosperity". Mundell in his The Sveriges Riksbank Prize in Economic Sciences in Memory of Alfred Nobel acceptance lecture (awarded for unrelated work in optimum currency area) countered that the success of price stability was proof that the supply-side revolution had worked. The continuing debate over supply-side policies tends to focus on the massive federal and current account deficits, increased income inequality and its failure to promote growth.

In 2006 Sebastian Mallaby of The Washington Post quoted George W. Bush, Dick Cheney, Bill Frist, Chuck Grassley, and Rick Santorum misstating the effect of the Bush Administration's tax cuts. On January 3, 2007, George W. Bush wrote an article claiming "It is also a fact that our tax cuts have fueled robust economic growth and record revenues."

Andrew Samwick, who was Chief Economist on Bush's Council of Economic Advisers from 2003-2004 responded to the claim:

> You are smart people. You know that the tax cuts have not fueled record revenues. You know what it takes to establish causality. You know that the first order effect of cutting taxes is to lower tax revenues. We all agree that the ultimate reduction in tax revenues can be less than this first order effect, because lower tax rates encourage greater economic activity and thus expand the tax base. No thoughtful person believes that this possible offset more than compensated for the first effect for these tax cuts. Not a single one.
>
> The Congressional Budget Office (CBO) has estimated that extending the Bush tax cuts of 2001-2003 beyond their 2010 expiration would increase deficits by $1.8 trillion dollars over the following decade. The CBO also completed a study in 2005 analyzing a hypothetical 10% income tax cut and concluded that under various scenarios there would be minimal offsets to the loss of revenue. In other words, deficits would increase by nearly the same amount as the tax cut in the first five years, with limited feedback revenue thereafter.

From time to time politicians make blunt claims that tax cuts increase goverment revenue (e.g. Mitch McConnell in July 2010) However, the Laffer Curve clearly shows that only cutting tax rates to the right of peak economic performance rate will increase revenues, and that cutting tax rates to the left of the peak rate will decrease revenues.

The paradigm of a tax system which rewards investment over consumption was accepted across the political spectrum, and no plan not rooted in supply-side economic theories has been advanced in the United States since 1982 (with the exception of the Clinton tax increases of 1993) which had any serious chance of passage into law. In 1986, a tax overhaul, described by Mundell as "the completion of the supply-side revolution" was drafted.

It included increases in payroll taxes, decreases in top marginal rates, and increases in capital gains taxes. Combined with the mortgage interest deduction and the regressive effects of state taxation, it produces closer to a flat-tax effect. Proponents, such as Mundell and Laffer, point to the dramatic rise in the stock market as a sign that the tax overhaul was effective, although they note that the hike in capital gains may be more trouble than it was worth. Cutting marginal tax rates can also be perceived as primarily beneficial to the wealthy, which commentators such as Paul Krugman see as politically rather than economically motivated.

> "The specific set of foolish ideas that has laid claim to the name "supply side economics" is a crank doctrine that would have had little influence if it did not appeal to the prejudices of editors and wealthy men."

Remarkably, John Kenneth Galbraith noted that supply side economics was not a new theory. He wrote, "Mr. David Stockman has said that supply-side economics was merely a cover for the trickle-down approach to economic policy—what an older and less elegant generation called the horse-and-sparrow theory: If you feed the horse enough oats, some will pass through to the road for the sparrows." Galbraith claimed that the horse and sparrow theory was partly to blame for the Panic of 1896.

Supply-siders blame the 1991 recession on the Federal

Reserve, and argue that Clinton's tax increases, since they did not change marginal capital gains tax rates, left the supply-side nature of the 1986 tax bill in place. Similarly, supply-side economists have argued that since the early phases of the massive tax breaks of George W. Bush's first two years were based on credits and not cuts in marginal rates, they did not act to stimulate the economy, although the effect on individual income remains the same. More generally, traditional economists point to the "overhang" of deficits from the Reagan Era, the S&L bailout, the effects of a ballooning federal budget deficit, the defense budget cuts which began in earnest in 1989, and the expectation of a lack of continued fiscal discipline as the source of the recession. These arguments blame the legacy of Democratic deficits forced upon Reagan, rather than deficits run up during Reagan's own administration.

Critics of supply-side economics often argue the inflated government deficits that accompanied the arrival of supply-side economics are of greater concern than the stock market success of supply-side theory.

In 2003, the *Wall Street Journal* declared the debate over supply-side economics to have ended "with a whimper" after extensive modeling performed by the Congressional Budget Office (CBO) failed to support the most extreme claims of supply-side policies. It was also suggested that Dan Crippen may have lost his chance at reappointment as head of the CBO for failing to support supply-side inspired dynamic scoring. This research undermines the claim that tax cuts can completely compensate for the initial loss of revenue due to the cut, but does acknowledge that resulting growth from the tax cut does replace some of the lost revenue, and the CBO has come under fire for using low estimates.

Before President Bush signed the 2003 tax cuts, the

progressive, nonpartisan Economic Policy Institute (EPI) released a statement signed by ten Nobel prize laureates entitled "Economists' statement opposing the Bush tax cuts", which states that:

> "Passing these tax cuts will worsen the long-term budget outlook, adding to the nation's projected chronic deficits. This fiscal deterioration will reduce the capacity of the government to finance Social Security and Medicare benefits as well as investments in schools, health, infrastructure, and basic research. Moreover, the proposed tax cuts will generate further inequalities in after-tax income."

Milton Friedman agreed the tax cuts would reduce tax revenues and result in intolerable deficits, though he supported them as a means to restrain federal spending. Friedman characterized the reduced government tax revenue as "cutting their allowance".

Later analysis of the Bush tax cuts by the Economic Policy Institute claims that the Bush tax cuts have failed to promote growth, as all macroeconomic growth indicators, save the housing market, were well below average for the 2001 to 2005 business cycle. These critics argue that the Bush tax cuts have done little more than deprive government of revenue, and increase deficit and after-tax income inequality.

In the two years since that report, though, growth has remained strong, and newer numbers dispute the conclusions of the EPI report. The Bush administration points to the long period of sustained growth, both in GDP and in overall job numbers, as well as increases in personal income and decreases in the government deficit. The results of the tax cuts in the U.S. in 2001 and 2003 are mixed. While results show a temporary decline in tax receipts, they later recovered due to economic growth. In this analysis, it is difficult to discern the reason for the decreases in tax revenue because

2001 was the same year that the dot-com bubble burst. Total Federal Revenues in FY2000 were $2,025 billion (in inflation adjusted dollars). In 2001, President George W. Bush signed the Economic Growth and Tax Relief Reconciliation Act of 2001. Rather than wait for the start of the new fiscal year, income tax rate reductions started on July 1, 2001. In addition, rebate checks were sent to everyone that filed a 2000 income tax return (before Oct 1, the start of the new federal fiscal year).

Federal revenues in FY2001 were $1,946 billion, $79 billion lower than in FY2000. More of the 2001 tax cut took effect at the start of FY2002, including cuts in the estate tax, retirement and educational savings. Federal revenues in FY2002 were $1,777 billion, $247 billion lower than in FY2000. In 2003, President Bush signed the Jobs and Growth Tax Relief Reconciliation Act of 2003. Income tax rates were immediately reduced and rebate checks issued (without waiting for the new fiscal year). Federal revenues in FY2003 were $1,665 billion, $360 billion lower than in FY2000. Federal revenues in FY2004 were 1,707 billion, $318 billion lower than in FY2000.

Federal revenues in FY2005 were $1,888, $137 billion lower than in FY2000, but by 2006 revenue had completely recovered (in inflation adjusted dollars), with receipts at $2,037 Billion, $12 billion higher than 2000. The cumulative total of federal revenues less than in FY2000 for the fiscal years 2001-2005 was $1.142 trillion, with that amount expected to be recovered by 2011, with 2012 expected to produce an additional $400 billion in excess revenue over 2000.

Federal revenues include revenue from different taxes that were cut, stayed the same, or were raised. For example, the Social Security FICA tax rate stayed the same while the maximum income subject to the tax was increased each year, resulting in a tax increase for those earning more than the previous limit. Social Security tax revenues increased each and every year. Including increasing tax revenues from taxes that stayed the same or were increased hides the magnitude of the revenue decrease in taxes that were cut. Income tax rates were cut and income tax revenues were lower than the FY2000 level each and every fiscal year from 2001–2005, a cumulative revenue decrease of $640 billion (measured in nominal dollars).

But, by 2006 revenues exceeded the 2000 level. Likewise Corporate income tax rates were cut and revenues were lower than the FY2000 level each and every fiscal year from 2001-2004. But, by 2005 the inflation adjusted take exceeded that of 2000 by over 20%, and by 2006 nearly 50% higher. In 2006, the CBO released a study titled "A Dynamic Analysis of Permanent Extension of the President's Tax Relief." This study found that under the best possible scenario, making tax cuts permanent would increase the economy "over the long run" by 0.7%.

Since the "long run" is not defined, some commentators have suggested that 20 years should be used, making the annual best case GDP growth equal to 0.04%. When compared with the cost of the tax cuts, the best case growth scenario is still not sufficient to pay for the tax cuts. Previous official CBO estimates had identified the tax cuts as costing the equivalent of 1.4% of the GDP in revenue. According to the study, if the best case growth scenario is applied, the tax cuts would still cost the equivalent of 1.27% of the GDP.

It is pertinent to note that this study was criticized by many economists, including Harvard Economics Professor Greg Mankiw, who pointed out that the CBO used a very low value for the earnings-weighted compensated labor supply elasticity of 0.14. In a paper published in the Journal of Public Economics, Mankiw and Matthew Weinzierl noted that the current economics research would place an appropriate value for labor supply elasticity at around 0.5, although Dr. Mankiw notes, "unfortunately, the academic literature on this topic is far from conclusive."

Remarkably, a recent working paper sponsored by the IMF showed "that the Laffer curve can arise even with very small changes in labor supply effects" but that "labor supply changes do not cause the Laffer effect." This is contrary to the supply-side explanation of the Laffer curve, in which the increases in tax revenue are held to be the result of an increase in labor supply.

Instead their proposed mechanism for the Laffer effect was that "tax rate cuts can increase revenues by improving tax compliance."

The study examined in particular the case of Russia which has comparatively high rates of tax evasion. In that case, their tax compliance model did yield significant revenue increases:

> "To illustrate the potential effects of tax rate cuts on tax revenues consider the example of Russia. Russia introduced a flat 13 percent personal income tax rate, replacing the three tiered, 12, 20 and 30 percent previous rates (as detailed in Ivanova, Keen and Klemm, 2005). The tax exempt income was also increased, further decreasing the tax burden. Considering social tax reforms enacted at the same time, tax rates were cut substantially for most taxpayers. However, personal income tax (PIT) revenues have increased significantly: 46 percent in nominal and 26 percent real terms during the next year. Even more interesting PIT revenues have increased from 2.4 percent to 2.9 percent of GDP—a more than 20 percent increase relative to GDP. PIT revenues continued to increase to 3.3

percent during the next year, representing a further 14 percent gain relative to GDP."

In this chapter we have put ample light on supply-side economics, citing cases from the US experience. In the next chapter we will discuss the issue of inflation.

REFERENCES

Alan Reynolds (July 1999). "Capital gains tax: Analysis of reform options for Australia" (PDF). Hudson Institute. http://www.asx.com.au/about/pdf/cgt.pdf.

Atkinson, Robert D. Supply-side Follies: Why Conservative Economics Fails, Liberal Economics Falters, and Innovation Economics Is the Answer. Lanham: Rowman & Littlefield, 2006. Print.

Bartlett, Bruce (2007-04-06). "How Supply-Side Economics Trickled Down". *New York Times*. http://www.nytimes.com/2007/04/06/opinion/06bartlett.html.

Bartlett, Bruce. "Supply-Side Economics: "Voodoo Economics" or Lasting Contribution?" (PDF). *Laffer Associates* (November 11, 2003). http://web.uconn.edu/cunningham/econ309/lafferpdf.pdf. Retrieved 2008-11-17.

Blinder, A. S. (2006). "Can fiscal policy improve macro-stabilization". In Kopcke, E.; Tootell, G. M. B.; Triest, R. K.. *The macroeconomics of fiscal policy*. Cambridge, MA: MIT Press. pp. 23–62.

Bouchard, Mike (12 Sept 2006). "A Rising Tide Lifts all Boats". townhall.com.

Brownlee, E. (2006). "Fiscal policy in the Reagan administration". In Kopcke, E.; Tootell. G. M. B.; Triest, R. K.. *The macroeconomics of fiscal policy*. Cambr*Italic text*idge, MA: MIT Press. pp. 117–204.

Bush, George W. (2007-01-03). "What the Congress Can Do for America". *Wall Street Journal*.

Canto, Victor (1983). "The Foundations of Supply-Side Economics". http://www.highbeam.com/doc/1G1-20004037.html.

Case, K. E.; Fair, R. C. (2007). *Principles of Economics* (8th ed.). Upper Saddle Rive, NJ: Prentice Hall.

Case, Karl E. & Fair, Ray C. (1999). *Principles of Economics* (5th ed.), p. 780. Prentice-Hall.

Chait, J. (2007). *The Big Con: How Washington Got Hoodwinked and Hijacked by Crackpot Economics*. Boston: Houghton Mifflin.

Dynamic' Scoring Finally Ends Debate On Taxes, Revenue. By Alan Murray. *Wall Street Journal.* (Eastern edition). New York, N.Y.: Apr 1, 2003. pg. A.4

Galbraith, John Kenneth (1982-02-04). "Recession Economics". *New York Review of Books*.

Gale, W. G. & Orszag, P. R. (2003-05-09). "Bush's Tax Plan Slashes Growth". The Brookings Institution. http://www.brookings.edu/views/op-ed/gale/20030509.htm. Retrieved 2007-10-23.

Krugman, Paul R. (2009). *The Return Of Depression Economics And The Crisis Of 2008*. W.W. Norton, p. 192.

Malabre, Jr., Alfred L. (1994). *Lost Prophets: An Insider's History of the Modern Economists*, p. 182. Harvard Business School Press.

Martin, Douglas (2005-08-31). "Jude Wanniski, 69, Journalist Who Coined the Term 'Supply-Side Economics,' Dies". *New York Times*. http://www.nytimes.com/2005/08/31/business/31wanniski.html.

Martin, Keith D. (2010). *A Liberal Mandate: Reflections on our Founding Vision and Rants on how we have Failed to Achieve it*. Silver Spring, MD: WeitPress.

Moore, Stephen (2003-02-28). "Think Twice About Gregory Mankiw". *National Review*.

Papp, TK and Takáts, E (PDF). *Tax rate cuts and tax compliance—the Laffer curve revisited*. IMF Working Paper.

Quote from Mankiw with source in Bartels, L. M. (2008). *Unequal democracy: The political-economy of the new gilded age*. Princeton, NJ: Princeton University Press.

Scheiber, Noam (2004-04-08). "Can Greg Mankiw Survive Politics?". *The New Republic*.

See p. 5: "Contradicting the traditional labor supply based explanation of the Laffer effect, measures of labor supply remained mostly unchanged."

Tobin, J. (1992). "Voodoo curse". *Harvard International Review* 14 (4): 10.

Wanniski, Jude (1978). *The Way the World Works: How Economies Fail—and Succeed*. New York: Basic Books.

Wanniski, Jude (1994). "Karl Marx Revisited". http://www.polyconomics.com/essays/esy-940124.htm.

5

Inflation

> "The survival of the fittest is the ageless law of nature, but the fittest are rarely the strong. The fittest are those endowed with the qualifications for adaptation, the ability to accept the inevitable and conform to the unavoidable, to harmonize the existing or changing conditions."
>
> —*Dane E. Smalley*

Inflation is bad as well as good for economic health of a nation. In economics, inflation is a rise in the general level of prices of goods and services in an economy over a period of time. When the general price level rises, each unit of currency buys fewer goods and services. Consequently, inflation also reflects an erosion in the purchasing power of money – a loss of real value in the internal medium of exchange and unit of account in the economy. A chief measure of price inflation is the inflation rate, the annualized percentage change in a general price index (normally the Consumer Price Index) over time.

It must be remembered that inflation's effects on an economy are various and can be simultaneously positive and negative. Negative effects of inflation include a decrease in the real value of money and other monetary items over time, uncertainty over future inflation may discourage investment and savings, and high inflation may lead to shortages of goods if consumers begin hoarding out of concern that prices will increase in the future. Positive effects include ensuring central banks can adjust nominal interest rates (intended to mitigate recessions), and encouraging investment in non-monetary capital projects.

Economists generally agree that high rates of inflation and hyperinflation are caused by an excessive growth of the money supply. Views on which factors determine low to moderate rates of inflation are more varied. Low or moderate inflation may be attributed to fluctuations in real demand for goods and services, or changes in available supplies such as during scarcities, as well as to growth in the money supply.

However, the consensus view is that a long sustained period of inflation is caused by money supply growing faster than the rate of economic growth.

Today, most mainstream economists favor a low, steady rate of inflation. Low (as opposed to zero or negative) inflation may reduce the severity of economic recessions by enabling the labor market to adjust more quickly in a downturn, and reduce the risk that a liquidity trap prevents monetary policy from stabilizing the economy. The task of keeping the rate of inflation low and stable is usually given to monetary authorities.

Generally, these monetary authorities are the central banks that control the size of the money supply through the setting of interest rates, through open market operations, and through the setting of banking reserve requirements.

Now we should have a look at history of inflation.

In fact, increases in the quantity of money or in the overall money supply (or debasement of the means of exchange) have occurred in many different societies throughout history, changing with different forms of money used. For instance, when gold was used as currency, the government could collect gold coins, melt them down, mix them with other metals such as silver, copper or lead, and reissue them at the same nominal value. By diluting the gold with other metals, the government could issue more coins without also needing to increase the amount of gold used to make them.

When the cost of each coin is lowered in this way, the government profits from an increase in seigniorage. This practice would increase the money supply but at the same time the relative value of each coin would be lowered. As the relative value of the coins becomes less, consumers would need to give more coins in exchange for the same goods and services as before. These goods and services would experience a price increase as the value of each coin is reduced.

Remarkably, from the second half of the 15th century to the first half of the 17th, Western Europe experienced a major inflationary cycle referred to as the "price revolution", with prices on average rising perhaps sixfold over 150 years. This was largely caused by the sudden influx of gold and silver from the New World into Habsburg Spain. The silver spread throughout a previously cash starved Europe, and caused widespread inflation.

Demographic factors also contributed to upward pressure on prices, with European population growth after depopulation caused by the Black Death pandemic. By the nineteenth century, economists categorized three separate factors that cause a rise or fall in the price of goods: a change in the *value* or resource costs of the good, a change in the *price of money* which then was usually a fluctuation in the commodity price of the metallic content in the currency, and *currency depreciation* resulting from an increased supply of currency relative to the quantity of redeemable metal backing the currency.

Following the proliferation of private bank note currency printed during the American Civil War, the term "inflation" started to appear as a direct reference to the *currency depreciation* that occurred as the quantity of redeemable bank notes outstripped the quantity of metal available for their redemption. The term inflation then referred to the devaluation of the currency, and not to a rise in the price of goods.

Notably, this relationship between the over-supply of bank notes and a resulting depreciation in their value was noted by earlier classical economists such as David Hume and David Ricardo, who would go on to examine and debate to what effect a currency devaluation (later termed *monetary inflation*) has on the price of goods (later termed *price inflation*, and eventually just *inflation*). The adoption of fiat currency (paper money) by many countries, from the 18th century onwards, made much larger variations in the supply of money possible.

Since then, huge increases in the supply of paper money have taken place in a number of countries, producing hyperinflations— episodes of extreme inflation rates much higher than those observed in earlier periods of commodity money. The hyperinflation suffered by the Weimar Republic of Germany is a notable example.

It is pertinent to note that the term "inflation" originally referred to increases in the amount of money in circulation, and some economists still use the word in this way. However, most economists today use the term "inflation" to refer to a rise in the price level. An increase in the money supply may be called monetary inflation, to distinguish it from rising prices, which may also for clarity be called 'price inflation'. Economists generally agree that in the long run, inflation is caused by increases in the money supply.

However, in the short and medium term, inflation is largely dependent on supply and demand pressures in the economy. Other economic concepts related to inflation include: deflation – a fall in the general price level; disinflation – a decrease in the rate of inflation; hyperinflation – an out-of-control inflationary spiral; stagflation – a combination of inflation, slow economic growth and high unemployment; and reflation – an attempt to raise the general level of prices to counteract deflationary pressures.

As such, since there are many possible measures of the price level, there are many possible measures of price inflation. Most frequently, the term "inflation" refers to a rise in a broad price index representing the overall price level for goods and services in the economy. The Consumer Price Index (CPI), the Personal Consumption Expenditures Price Index (PCEPI) and the GDP deflator are some examples of broad price indices. However, "inflation" may also be used to describe a rising price level within a narrower set of assets, goods or services within the economy, such as commodities (including food, fuel, metals), financial assets (such as stocks, bonds and real estate), services (such as entertainment and health care), or labor.

The Reuters-CRB Index (CCI), the Producer Price Index, and Employment Cost Index (ECI) are examples of narrow price indices used to measure price inflation in particular sectors of the economy. Core inflation is a measure of inflation for a subset of consumer prices that excludes food and energy prices, which rise and fall more than other prices in the short term. The Federal Reserve Board pays particular attention to the core inflation rate to get a better estimate of long-term future inflation trends overall.

Measures of Inflation

It is pertinent to note that inflation is usually estimated by calculating the inflation rate of a price index, usually the Consumer Price Index. The Consumer Price Index measures prices of a selection of goods and services purchased by a "typical consumer". The inflation rate is the percentage rate of change of a price index over time.

Price Indices for Calculating Price Inflation

- Producer price indices (PPIs) which measures average changes in prices received by domestic producers for their output. This differs from the CPI in that price subsidization, profits, and taxes may cause the amount received by the producer to differ from what the consumer paid. There is also typically a delay between an increase in the PPI and any eventual increase in the CPI. Producer price index measures the pressure being put on producers by the costs of their raw materials. This could be "passed on" to consumers, or it could be absorbed by profits, or offset by increasing productivity. In India and the United States, an earlier version of the PPI was called the Wholesale Price Index.
- Commodity price indices, which measure the price of a selection of commodities. In the present commodity price indices are weighted by the relative importance of the components to the "all in" cost of an employee.
- Core price indices: because food and oil prices can change quickly due to changes in supply and demand conditions in the food and oil markets, it can be difficult to detect the long run trend in price levels when those prices are included. Therefore most statistical agencies also report a measure of 'core inflation', which removes the most volatile components (such as food and oil) from a broad price index like the CPI. Because core inflation is less affected by short run supply and demand conditions in specific markets, central banks rely on it to better measure the inflationary impact of current monetary policy.

For instance, in January 2007, the U.S. Consumer Price Index was 202.416, and in January 2008 it was 211.080.

Remarkably, the resulting inflation rate for the CPI in this one year period is 4.28%, meaning the general level of prices for typical U.S. consumers rose by approximately four percent in 2007.

Other common measures of inflation are:

- GDP deflator is a measure of the price of all the goods and services included in Gross Domestic Product (GDP). The US Commerce Department publishes a deflator series for US GDP, defined as its nominal GDP measure divided by its real GDP measure.
- Regional inflation The Bureau of Labor Statistics breaks down CPI-U calculations down to different regions of the US.
- Historical inflation Before collecting consistent econometric data became standard for governments, and for the purpose of comparing absolute, rather than relative standards of living, various economists have calculated imputed inflation figures. Most inflation data before the early 20th century is imputed based on the known costs of goods, rather than compiled at the time. It is also used to adjust for the differences in real standard of living for the presence of technology.
- Asset price inflation is an undue increase in the prices of real or financial assets, such as stock (equity) and real estate. While there is no widely accepted index of this type, some central bankers have suggested that it would be better to aim at stabilizing a wider general price level inflation

measure that includes some asset prices, instead of stabilizing CPI or core inflation only. The reason is that by raising interest rates when stock prices or real estate prices rise, and lowering them when these asset prices fall, central banks might be more successful in avoiding bubbles and crashes in asset prices.

It must be remembered that measuring inflation in an economy requires objective means of differentiating changes in nominal prices on a common set of goods and services, and distinguishing them from those price shifts resulting from changes in value such as volume, quality, or performance. For example, if the price of a 10 oz. can of corn changes from $0.90 to $1.00 over the course of a year, with no change in quality, then this price difference represents inflation. This single price change would not, however, represent general inflation in an overall economy. To measure overall inflation, the price change of a large "basket" of representative goods and services is measured. This is the purpose of a price index, which is the combined price of a "basket" of many goods and services.

The combined price is the sum of the weighted average prices of items in the "basket". A weighted price is calculated by multiplying the unit price of an item to the number of those items the average consumer purchases. Weighted pricing is a necessary means to measuring the impact of individual unit price changes on the economy's overall inflation. The Consumer Price Index, for example, uses data collected by surveying households to determine what proportion of the typical consumer's overall spending is spent on specific goods and services, and weights the average prices of those items accordingly.

Those weighted average prices are combined to calculate the overall price. To better relate price changes over time, indexes typically choose a "base year" price and assign it a value of 100. Index prices in subsequent years are then expressed in relation to the base year price. Inflation measures are often modified over time, either for the relative weight of goods in the basket, or in the way in which goods and services from the present are compared with goods and services from the past. Over time adjustments are made to the type of goods and services selected in order to reflect changes in the sorts of goods and services purchased by 'typical consumers'.

New products may be introduced, older products disappear, the quality of existing products may change, and consumer preferences can shift. Both the sorts of goods and services which are included in the "basket" and the weighted price used in inflation measures will be changed over time in order to keep pace with the changing marketplace. Inflation numbers are often seasonally adjusted in order to differentiate expected cyclical cost shifts. For example, home heating costs are expected to rise in colder months, and seasonal adjustments are often used when measuring for inflation to compensate for cyclical spikes in energy or fuel demand.

Inflation numbers may be averaged or otherwise subjected to statistical techniques in order to remove statistical noise and volatility of individual prices. When looking at inflation economic institutions may focus only on certain kinds of prices, or *special indices*, such as the core inflation index which is used by central banks to formulate monetary policy.

Most inflation indices are calculated from weighted averages of selected price changes. This necessarily introduces distortion, and can lead to legitimate disputes about what the true inflation rate is. This problem can be overcome by including all available price changes in the calculation, and then choosing the median value.

Main Impacts

Notably, an increase in the general level of prices implies a decrease in the purchasing power of the currency. That is, when the general level of prices rises, each monetary unit buys fewer goods and services. The effect of inflation is not distributed evenly in the economy, and as a consequence there are hidden costs to some and benefits to others from this decrease in the purchasing power of money. For example, with inflation, lenders or depositors who are paid a fixed rate of interest on loans or deposits will lose purchasing power from their interest earnings, while their borrowers benefit.

Individuals or institutions with cash assets will experience a decline in the purchasing power of their holdings. Increases in payments to workers and pensioners often lag behind inflation, especially for those with fixed payments. Increases in the price level (inflation) erode the real value of money (the functional currency) and other items with an underlying monetary nature (e.g. loans and bonds). However, inflation has no effect on the real value of non-monetary items, (e.g. goods and commodities, gold, real estate). Debtors who have debts with a fixed nominal rate of interest will see a reduction in the "real" interest rate as the inflation rate rises. The "real" interest on a loan is the nominal rate minus the inflation rate (approximately).

For example if you take a loan where the stated interest rate is 6% and the inflation rate is at 3%, the real interest rate that you are paying for the loan is 3%. It would also hold true that if you had a loan at a fixed interest rate of 6% and the inflation rate jumped to 20% you would have a real interest rate of -14%. Banks and other lenders adjust for this inflation risk either by including an inflation premium in the costs of lending the money by creating a higher initial stated interest rate or by setting the interest at a variable rate. As the rate of inflation decreases, this has the opposite (negative) effect on borrowers.

High or unpredictable inflation rates are regarded as harmful to an overall economy. They add inefficiencies in the market, and make it difficult for companies to budget or plan long-term. Inflation can act as a drag on productivity as companies are forced to shift resources away from products and services in order to focus on profit and losses from currency inflation. Uncertainty about the future purchasing power of money discourages investment and saving. And inflation can impose hidden tax increases, as inflated earnings push taxpayers into higher income tax rates unless the tax brackets are indexed to inflation. With high inflation, purchasing power is redistributed from those on fixed nominal incomes, such as some pensioners whose pensions are not indexed to the price level, towards those with variable incomes whose earnings may better keep pace with the inflation.

This redistribution of purchasing power will also occur between international trading partners. Where fixed exchange rates are imposed, higher inflation in one economy than another will cause the first economy's exports to become more expensive and affect the balance of trade. There can also be negative impacts to trade from an increased instability in currency exchange prices caused by unpredictable inflation.

Types of Inflation

1. Cost-push Inflation

High inflation can prompt employees to demand rapid

wage increases, to keep up with consumer prices. In the cost-push theory of inflation, rising wages in turn can help fuel inflation. In the case of collective bargaining, wage growth will be set as a function of inflationary expectations, which will be higher when inflation is high. This can cause a wage spiral. In a sense, inflation begets further inflationary expectations, which beget further inflation.

2. Hoarding

People buy durable and/or non-perishable commodities and other goods as stores of wealth, to avoid the losses expected from the declining purchasing power of money, creating shortages of the hoarded goods.

3. Social Unrest and Revolts

Inflation can lead to massive demonstrations and revolutions. For example, inflation and in particular food inflation is considered as one of the main reasons that caused 2010–2011 Tunisian revolution and Egyptian Revolution of 2011, according to many observators including Robert Zoellick, president of the World Bank. Tunisian president Zine El Abidine Ben Ali was ousted, Egyptian President Hosni Mubarak was also ousted after only 18 days of demonstrations, and protests soon spread in many countries of North Africa and Middle East.

4. Hyperinflation

If inflation gets totally out of control (in the upward direction), it can grossly interfere with the normal workings of the economy, hurting its ability to supply goods. Hyperinflation can lead to the abandonment of the use of the country's currency, leading to the inefficiencies of barter.

5. Allocative Efficiency

A change in the supply or demand for a good will normally cause its relative price to change, signaling to buyers and sellers that they should re-allocate resources in response to the new market conditions. But when prices are constantly changing due to inflation, price changes due to genuine relative price signals are difficult to distinguish from price changes due to general inflation, so agents are slow to respond to them. The result is a loss of allocative efficiency.

6. Shoe Leather Cost

High inflation increases the opportunity cost of holding cash balances and can induce people to hold a greater portion of their assets in interest paying accounts. However, since cash is still needed in order to carry out transactions this means that more "trips to the bank" are necessary in order to make withdrawals, proverbially wearing out the "shoe leather" with each trip.

Menu Costs

With high inflation, firms must change their prices often in order to keep up with economy-wide changes. But often changing prices is itself a costly activity whether explicitly, as with the need to print new menus, or implicitly.

Business Cycles

According to the Austrian Business Cycle Theory, inflation sets off the business cycle. Austrian economists hold this to be the most damaging effect of inflation. According to Austrian theory, artificially low interest rates and the associated increase in the money supply lead to reckless, speculative borrowing, resulting in clusters of malinvestments, which eventually have to be liquidated as they become unsustainable.

Positive

Labor-Market Adjustments

Keynesians believe that nominal wages are slow to

adjust downwards. This can lead to prolonged disequilibrium and high unemployment in the labor market. Since inflation would lower the real wage if nominal wages are kept constant, Keynesians argue that some inflation is good for the economy, as it would allow labor markets to reach equilibrium faster.

Room to Maneuver

The primary tools for controlling the money supply are the ability to set the discount rate, the rate at which banks can borrow from the central bank, and open market operations which are the central bank's interventions into the bonds market with the aim of affecting the nominal interest rate. If an economy finds itself in a recession with already low, or even zero, nominal interest rates, then the bank cannot cut these rates further (since negative nominal interest rates are impossible) in order to stimulate the economy - this situation is known as a liquidity trap. A moderate level of inflation tends to ensure that nominal interest rates stay sufficiently above zero so that if the need arises the bank can cut the nominal interest rate.

Mundell-Tobin Effect

The Nobel laureate Robert Mundell noted that moderate inflation would induce savers to substitute lending for some money holding as a means to finance future spending. That substitution would cause market clearing real interest rates to fall. The lower real rate of interest would induce more borrowing to finance investment.

In a similar vein, Nobel laureate James Tobin noted that such inflation would cause businesses to substitute investment in physical capital (plant, equipment, and inventories) for money balances in their asset portfolios. That substitution would mean choosing the making of investments with lower rates of real return. (The rates of return are lower because the investments with higher rates of return were already being made before.)

The two related effects are known as the Mundell-Tobin effect. Unless the economy is already overinvesting according to models of economic growth theory, that extra investment resulting from the effect would be seen as positive.

Instability with Deflation

Economist S.C. Tsaing noted that once substantial deflation is expected, two important effects will appear; both a result of money holding substituting for lending as a vehicle for saving. The first was that continually falling prices and the resulting incentive to hoard money will cause instability resulting from the likely increasing fear, while money hoards grow in value, that the value of those hoards are at risk, as people realize that a movement to trade those money hoards for real goods and assets will quickly drive those prices up.

Any movement to spend those hoards "once started would become a tremendous avalanche, which could rampage for a long time before it would spend itself." Thus, a regime of long-term deflation is likely to be interrupted by periodic spikes of rapid inflation and consequent real economic disruptions. Moderate and stable inflation would avoid such a seesawing of price movements.

Financial Market Inefficiency with Deflation

The second effect noted by Tsaing is that when savers have substituted money holding for lending on financial markets, the role of those markets in channeling savings into investment is undermined. With nominal interest rates driven to zero, or near zero, from the competition with a high return money asset, there would be no price mechanism in whatever is left of those markets. With financial markets effectively euthanized, the remaining goods and physical asset prices would move in perverse directions. For example, an increased desire to save could not push interest rates further down (and thereby stimulate investment) but would instead cause additional money hoarding, driving consumer prices further down and making investment in consumer goods production thereby less attractive. Moderate inflation, once its expectation is incorporated into nominal interest rates, would give those interest rates room to go both up and down in response to shifting investment opportunities, or savers' preferences, and thus allow financial markets to function in a more normal fashion.

Causes of Inflation

Historically, a great deal of economic literature was concerned with the question of what causes inflation and what effect it has. There were different schools of thought as to the causes of inflation. Most can be divided into two broad areas: quality theories of inflation and quantity theories of inflation. The quality theory of inflation rests on the expectation of a seller accepting currency to be able to exchange that currency at a later time for goods that are desirable as a buyer.

The quantity theory of inflation rests on the quantity equation of money, that relates the money supply, its velocity, and the nominal value of exchanges. Adam Smith and David Hume proposed a quantity theory of inflation for money, and a quality theory of inflation for production. Currently, the quantity theory of money is widely accepted as an accurate model of inflation in the long run. Consequently, there is now broad agreement among economists that in the long run, the inflation rate is essentially dependent on the growth rate of money supply.

However, in the short and medium term inflation may

be affected by supply and demand pressures in the economy, and influenced by the relative elasticity of wages, prices and interest rates. The question of whether the short-term effects last long enough to be important is the central topic of debate between monetarist and Keynesian economists. In monetarism prices and wages adjust quickly enough to make other factors merely marginal behavior on a general trend-line. In the Keynesian view, prices and wages adjust at different rates, and these differences have enough effects on real output to be "long term" in the view of people in an economy.

Keynesian economic theory proposes that changes in money supply do not directly affect prices, and that visible inflation is the result of pressures in the economy expressing themselves in prices. The supply of money is a major, but not the only, cause of inflation.

There are three major types of inflation, as part of what Robert J. Gordon calls the "triangle model":

- *Demand-pull inflation* is caused by increases in aggregate demand due to increased private and government spending, etc. Demand inflation is constructive to a faster rate of economic growth since the excess demand and favourable market conditions will stimulate investment and expansion.
- *Cost-push inflation*, also called "supply shock inflation," is caused by a drop in aggregate supply (potential output). This may be due to natural disasters, or increased prices of inputs. For example, a sudden decrease in the supply of oil, leading to increased oil prices, can cause cost-push inflation. Producers for whom oil is a part of their costs could then pass this on to consumers in the form of increased prices.

- Built-in inflation is induced by adaptive expectations, and is often linked to the "price/wage spiral". It involves workers trying to keep their wages up with prices (above the rate of inflation), and firms passing these higher labor costs on to their customers as higher prices, leading to a 'vicious circle'. Built-in inflation reflects events in the past, and so might be seen as hangover inflation.

It is apt to mention that demand-pull theory states that the rate of inflation accelerates whenever aggregate demand is increased beyond the ability of the economy to produce (its potential output). Hence, any factor that increases aggregate demand can cause inflation. However, in the long run, aggregate demand can be held above productive capacity only by increasing the quantity of money in circulation faster than the real growth rate of the economy.

Another (although much less common) cause can be a rapid decline in the *demand* for money, as happened in Europe during the Black Death, or in the Japanese occupied territories just before the defeat of Japan in 1945. The effect of money on inflation is most obvious when governments finance spending in a crisis, such as a civil war, by printing money excessively. This sometimes leads to hyperinflation, a condition where prices can double in a month or less.

Money supply is also thought to play a major role in determining moderate levels of inflation, although there are differences of opinion on how important it is. For example, Monetarist economists believe that the link is very strong; Keynesian economists, by contrast, typically emphasize the role of aggregate demand in the economy rather than the money supply in determining inflation.

That is, for Keynesians, the money supply is only one

determinant of aggregate demand. Some Keynesian economists also disagree with the notion that central banks fully control the money supply, arguing that central banks have little control, since the money supply adapts to the demand for bank credit issued by commercial banks. This is known as the theory of endogenous money, and has been advocated strongly by post-Keynesians as far back as the 1960s.

It has today become a central focus of Taylor rule advocates. This position is not universally accepted – banks create money by making loans, but the aggregate volume of these loans diminishes as real interest rates increase. Thus, central banks can influence the money supply by making money cheaper or more expensive, thus increasing or decreasing its production. A fundamental concept in inflation analysis is the relationship between inflation and unemployment, called the Phillips curve. This model suggests that there is a trade-off between price stability and employment.

Therefore, some level of inflation could be considered desirable in order to minimize unemployment. The Phillips curve model described the U.S. experience well in the 1960s but failed to describe the combination of rising inflation and economic stagnation (sometimes referred to as *stagflation*) experienced in the 1970s.

Thus, modern macroeconomics describes inflation using a Phillips curve that *shifts* (so the trade-off between inflation and unemployment changes) because of such matters as supply shocks and inflation becoming built into the normal workings of the economy. The former refers to such events as the oil shocks of the 1970s, while the latter refers to the price/wage spiral and inflationary expectations implying that the economy "normally" suffers from inflation.

Thus, the Phillips curve represents only the demand-pull component of the triangle model. Another concept of note is the potential output (sometimes called the "natural gross domestic product"), a level of GDP, where the economy is at its optimal level of production given institutional and natural constraints. (This level of output corresponds to the Non-Accelerating Inflation Rate of Unemployment, NAIRU, or the "natural" rate of unemployment or the full-employment unemployment rate.)

If GDP exceeds its potential (and unemployment is below the NAIRU), the theory says that inflation will *accelerate* as suppliers increase their prices and built-in inflation worsens. If GDP falls below its potential level (and unemployment is above the NAIRU), inflation will *decelerate* as suppliers attempt to fill excess capacity, cutting prices and undermining built-in inflation. However, one problem with this theory for policy-making purposes is that the exact level of potential output (and of the NAIRU) is generally unknown and tends to change over time. Inflation also seems to act in an asymmetric way, rising more quickly than it falls.

Worse, it can change because of policy: for example, high unemployment under British Prime Minister Margaret Thatcher might have led to a rise in the NAIRU (and a fall in potential) because many of the unemployed found themselves as structurally unemployed (also see unemployment), unable to find jobs that fit their skills.

A rise in structural unemployment implies that a smaller percentage of the labor force can find jobs at the NAIRU, where the economy avoids crossing the threshold into the realm of accelerating inflation.

Monetarist View

Monetarists believe the most significant factor

influencing inflation or deflation is how fast the money supply grows or shrinks. They consider fiscal policy, or government spending and taxation, as ineffective in controlling inflation. According to the famous monetarist economist Milton Friedman, *"Inflation is always and everywhere a monetary phenomenon."* Some monetarists, however, will qualify this by making an exception for very short-term circumstances.

Monetarists assert that the empirical study of monetary history shows that inflation has always been a monetary phenomenon. The quantity theory of money, simply stated, says that any change the amount of money in a system will change the price level. This theory begins with the equation of exchange:

$$MV = PQ$$

where

M is the nominal quantity of money.

V is the velocity of money in final expenditures;

P is the general price level;

Q is an index of the real value of final expenditures;

In this formula, the general price level is related to the level of real economic activity (Q), the quantity of money (M) and the velocity of money (V). The formula is an identity because the velocity of money (V) is defined to be the ratio of final nominal expenditure (PQ) to the quantity of money (M).

Monetarists assume that the velocity of money is unaffected by monetary policy (at least in the long run), and the real value of output is determined in the long run by the productive capacity of the economy. Under these assumptions, the primary driver of the change in the general price level is changes in the quantity of money.

With exogenous velocity (that is, velocity being determined externally and not being influenced by monetary policy), the money supply determines the value of nominal output (which equals final expenditure) in the short run. In practice, velocity is not exogenous in the short run, and so the formula does not necessarily imply a stable short-run relationship between the money supply and nominal output. However, in the long run, changes in velocity are assumed to be determined by the evolution of the payments mechanism.

If velocity is relatively unaffected by monetary policy, the long-run rate of increase in prices (the inflation rate) is equal to the long run growth rate of the money supply plus the exogenous long-run rate of velocity growth minus the long run growth rate of real output.

Unemployment

A connection between inflation and unemployment has been drawn since the emergence of large scale unemployment in the 19th century, and connections continue to be drawn today. In Marxian economics, the unemployed serve as a reserve army of labour, which restrain wage inflation. In the 20th century, similar concepts in Keynesian economics include the NAIRU (Non-Accelerating Inflation Rate of Unemployment) and the Phillips curve.

Rational Expectations Theory

Rational expectations theory holds that economic factors look rationally into the future when trying to maximize their well-being, and do not respond solely to immediate opportunity costs and pressures.

In this view, while generally grounded in monetarism, future expectations and strategies are important for inflation as well. A core assertion of rational expectations theory is that actors will seek to "head off" central-bank decisions by acting in ways that fulfill predictions of higher inflation. This means that central banks must establish their credibility in fighting inflation, or economic actors will make bets that the central bank will expand the money supply rapidly enough to prevent recession, even at the expense of exacerbating inflation.

Thus, if a central bank has a reputation as being "soft" on inflation, when it announces a new policy of fighting inflation with restrictive monetary growth economic agents will not believe that the policy will persist; their inflationary expectations will remain high, and so will inflation.

On the other hand, if the central bank has a reputation of being "tough" on inflation, then such a policy announcement will be believed and inflationary expectations will come down rapidly, thus allowing inflation itself to come down rapidly with minimal economic disruption.

Austrian View

The Austrian School asserts that inflation is an increase in the money supply, rising prices are merely consequences and this semantic difference is important in defining inflation. Austrians stress that inflation affects prices in various degree, i.e. that prices rise more sharply in some sectors than in other sectors of the economy.

The reason for the disparity is that excess money will be concentrated to certain sectors, such as housing, stocks or health care. Because of this disparity, Austrians argue that the aggregate price level can be very misleading when observing the effects of inflation. Austrian economists measure inflation by calculating the growth of new units of money that are available for immediate use in exchange, that have been created over time.

Real Bills Doctrine

Within the context of a fixed specie basis for money, one important controversy was between the quantity theory of money and the real bills doctrine (RBD). Within this context, quantity theory applies to the level of fractional reserve accounting allowed against specie, generally gold, held by a bank. Currency and banking schools of economics argue the RBD, that banks should also be able to issue currency against bills of trading, which is "real bills" that they buy from merchants.

This theory was important in the 19th century in debates between "Banking" and "Currency" schools of monetary soundness, and in the formation of the Federal Reserve. In the wake of the collapse of the international gold standard post 1913, and the move towards deficit financing of government, RBD has remained a minor topic, primarily of interest in limited contexts, such as currency boards. It is generally held in ill repute today, with Frederic Mishkin, a governor of the Federal Reserve going so far as to say it had been "completely discredited."

Remarkably, the debate between currency, or quantity theory, and banking schools in Britain during the 19th century prefigures current questions about the credibility of money in the present. In the 19th century the banking school had greater influence in policy in the United States and Great Britain, while the currency school had more influence "on the continent", that is in non-British countries, particularly in the Latin Monetary Union and the earlier Scandinavia monetary union.

Anti-classical or Backing Theory

Another issue associated with classical political economy is the anti-classical hypothesis of money, or "backing theory". The backing theory argues that the value of money is determined by the assets and liabilities of the issuing agency. Unlike the Quantity Theory of classical political economy, the backing theory argues that issuing authorities can issue money without causing inflation so long as the money issuer has sufficient assets to cover redemptions. There are very few backing theorists, making quantity theory the dominant theory explaining inflation.

How to Control Inflation?

In fact, a variety of methods have been used in attempts to control inflation.

1. Monetary Policy: Today the primary tool for controlling inflation is monetary policy. Most central banks are tasked with keeping the federal funds lending rate at a low level, normally to a target rate around 2% to 3% per annum, and within a targeted low inflation range, somewhere from about 2% to 6% per annum.

A low positive inflation is usually targeted, as deflationary conditions are seen as dangerous for the health of the economy. There are a number of methods that have been suggested to control inflation. Central banks such as the U.S. Federal Reserve can affect inflation to a significant extent through setting interest rates and through other operations.

High interest rates and slow growth of the money supply are the traditional ways through which central banks fight or prevent inflation, though they have different approaches. For instance, some follow a symmetrical inflation target while others only control inflation when it rises above a target, whether express or implied. Monetarists emphasize keeping the growth rate of money steady, and using monetary policy to control inflation (increasing interest rates, slowing the rise in the money supply).

Keynesians emphasize reducing aggregate demand during economic expansions and increasing demand during recessions to keep inflation stable. Control of aggregate demand can be achieved using both monetary policy and fiscal policy (increased taxation or reduced government spending to reduce demand).

2. Fixed Exchange Rates: Under a fixed exchange rate currency regime, a country's currency is tied in value to another single currency or to a basket of other currencies (or sometimes to another measure of value, such as gold). A fixed exchange rate is usually used to stabilize the value of a currency, vis-a-vis the currency it is pegged to. It can also be used as a means to control inflation.

However, as the value of the reference currency rises and falls, so does the currency pegged to it. This essentially means that the inflation rate in the fixed exchange rate country is determined by the inflation rate of the country the currency is pegged to. In addition, a fixed exchange rate prevents a government from using domestic monetary policy in order to achieve macroeconomic stability. Under the Bretton Woods agreement, most countries around the world had currencies that were fixed to the US dollar.

This limited inflation in those countries, but also exposed them to the danger of speculative attacks. After the Bretton Woods agreement broke down in the early 1970s, countries gradually turned to floating exchange rates. However, in the later part of the 20th century, some countries reverted to a fixed exchange rate as part of an attempt to control inflation.

This policy of using a fixed exchange rate to control inflation was used in many countries in South America in the later part of the 20th century (e.g. Argentina (1991-2002), Bolivia, Brazil, and Chile).

*3. **Gold Standard:*** The gold standard is a monetary system in which a region's common media of exchange are paper notes that are normally freely convertible into pre-set, fixed quantities of gold. The standard specifies how the gold backing would be implemented, including the amount of specie per currency unit.

The currency itself has no *innate value*, but is accepted by traders because it can be redeemed for the equivalent specie. A U.S. silver certificate, for example, could be redeemed for an actual piece of silver. The gold standard was partially abandoned via the international adoption of the Bretton Woods System. Under this system all other major currencies were tied at fixed rates to the dollar, which itself was tied to gold at the rate of $35 per ounce. The Bretton Woods system broke down in 1971, causing most countries to switch to fiat money – money backed only by the laws of the country.

It must be remembered that the under a gold standard, the long term rate of inflation (or deflation) would be determined by the growth rate of the supply of gold relative to total output. Critics argue that this will cause arbitrary fluctuations in the inflation rate, and that monetary policy would essentially be determined by gold mining, which some believe contributed to the Great Depression.

*4. **Wage and Price Controls:*** Another method attempted in the past have been wage and price controls ("incomes policies"). Wage and price controls have been successful in wartime environments in combination with rationing. However, their use in other contexts is far more mixed. Notable failures of their use include the 1972 imposition of wage and price controls by Richard Nixon. More successful examples include the Prices and Incomes Accord in Australia and the Wassenaar Agreement in the Netherlands. In general wage and price controls are regarded as a temporary and exceptional measure, only effective when coupled with policies designed to reduce the underlying causes of inflation during the wage and price control regime, for example, winning the war being fought. They often have perverse effects, due to the distorted signals they send to the market.

Artificially low prices often cause rationing and shortages and discourage future investment, resulting in yet further shortages. The usual economic analysis is that any product or service that is under-priced is overconsumed.

For example, if the official price of bread is too low, there will be too little bread at official prices, and too little investment in bread making by the market to satisfy future needs, thereby exacerbating the problem in the long term.

Remarkably, temporary controls may *complement* a recession as a way to fight inflation: the controls make the recession more efficient as a way to fight inflation (reducing the need to increase unemployment), while the recession prevents the kinds of distortions that controls cause when demand is high. However, in general the advice of economists is not to impose price controls but to liberalize prices by assuming that the economy will adjust and abandon unprofitable economic activity.

The lower activity will place fewer demands on whatever commodities were driving inflation, whether labor or resources, and inflation will fall with total economic output. This often produces a severe recession, as productive capacity is reallocated and is thus often very unpopular with the people whose livelihoods are destroyed.

Many economists and compensation analysts consider the idea of predetermined future "cost of living increases" to be misleading for two reasons: (1) For most recent periods in the industrialized world, average wages have increased faster than most calculated cost-of-living indexes, reflecting the influence of rising productivity and worker bargaining power rather than simply living costs, and (2) most cost-of-living indexes are not forward-looking, but instead compare current or historical data.

It is apt to mention that the real purchasing-power of fixed payments is eroded by inflation unless they are inflation-adjusted to keep their real values constant. In many countries, employment contracts, pension benefits, and government entitlements (such as social security) are tied to a cost-of-living index, typically to the consumer price index.

A *cost-of-living allowance* (COLA) adjusts salaries based on changes in a cost-of-living index. Salaries are typically adjusted annually in low inflation economies. During hyperinflation they are adjusted more often. They may also be tied to a cost-of-living index that varies by geographic location if the employee moves. Annual escalation clauses in employment contracts can specify retroactive or future percentage increases in worker pay which are not tied to any index. These negotiated increases in pay are colloquially referred to as cost-of-living adjustments or cost-of-living increases because of their similarity to increases tied to externally determined indexes.

After having a thorough understanding of inflation in this chapter, now we will turn to 'Recession' in the next chapter.

REFERENCES

Abel, Andrew; Bernanke, Ben (2005). *Macroeconomics* (5th ed.). Pearson

Barro, Robert J. (1997). *Macroeconomics*. Cambridge, Mass: MIT Press. pp. 895.

Baumol, William J. and Alan S. Blinder, *Macroeconomics: Principles and Policy*, Tenth edition. Thomson South-Western, 2006.

Blanchard, Olivier (2000). *Macroeconomics* (2nd ed.). Englewood Cliffs, N.J: Prentice Hall.

Burda, Michael C.; Wyplosz, Charles (1997). *Macroeconomics: a European text*. Oxford [Oxfordshire]: Oxford University Press.

Federal Reserve Bank of Boston, "Understanding Inflation and the Implications for Monetary Policy: A Phillips Curve Retrospective", *Conference Series 53*, June 9–11, 2008, Chatham, Massachusetts.

Hall, Robert E.; Taylor, John B. (1993). *Macroeconomics*. New York: W.W. Norton. pp. 637.

Leonardo Auernheimer, "The Honest Government's Guide to the Revenue From the Creation of Money," Journal of Political Economy, Vol. 82, No. 3, May/June 1974, pp. 598-606.

Mankiw, N. Gregory (2002). *Macroeconomics* (5th ed.). Worth

Mishkin, Frederic S., *The Economics of Money, Banking, and Financial Markets*, New York, Harper Collins, 1995.

Nenovsky. N, (2007), "Exchange Rate and Inflation: France and Bulgaria in the Interwar Period and the Contribution of Albert Aftalion (1874-1956)". *Bulgarian National Bank,* (2006)

Vasudevan, Ramaa, "What is the relation between inflation and unemployment?", in *Dollars & Sense*, September/October 2006.

6

Recession

"Life affords no higher pleasure than that of surmounting difficulties, passing from one step of success to another, forming new wishes and seeing them gratified. He that labors in any great or laudable undertaking has his fatigues first supported by hope and afterward rewarded by joy."

—Dr. Samuel Johnson

In common parlance in economics, by recession we mean a business cycle contraction, a general slowdown in economic activity. During recessions, many macroeconomic indicators vary in a similar way. Production, as generally, measured by Gross Domestic Product (GDP), employment, investment spending, capacity utilization, household incomes, business profits and inflation all fall during recessions; while bankruptcies and the unemployment rate rise unexpectedly.

It is pertinent to note that ecessions generally occur when there is a widespread drop in spending often following an adverse supply shock or the bursting of an economic bubble. Governments usually respond to recessions by adopting expansionary macroeconomic policies, such as increasing money supply, increasing government spending and decreasing taxation.

Now a look at different definitions of 'recession'.

There is no commonly accepted definition of a global

recession, although the IMF regards periods when global growth is less than 3% to be global recessions. The IMF estimates that global recessions seem to occur over a cycle lasting between 8 and 10 years. During what the IMF terms the past three global recessions of the last three decades, global per capita output growth was zero or negative.

Economists at the International Monetary Fund (IMF) state that a global recession would take a slowdown in global growth to three percent or less. By this measure, four periods since 1985 qualify: 1990–1993, 1998, 2001–2002 and 2008–2009.

Definition

Julius Shiskin in a 1975 *New York Times* article, economic statistician suggested several rules of thumb for defining a recession, one of which was "two down quarters of GDP". In time, the other rules of thumb were forgotten. Some economists prefer a definition of a 1.5% rise in unemployment within 12 months.

Remarkably, the United States, the Business Cycle Dating Committee of the National Bureau of Economic Research (NBER) is generally seen as the authority for dating US recessions. The NBER defines an economic recession as: "a significant decline in [the] economic activity spread across the country, lasting more than a few months, normally visible in real GDP growth, real personal income, employment (non-farm payrolls), industrial production, and wholesale-retail sales." Almost universally, academics, economists, policy makers, and businesses defer to the determination by the NBER for the precise dating of a recession's onset and end.

Main Attributes of Recession

In fact, a recession has many attributes that can occur simultaneously and includes declines in component measures of economic activity (GDP) such as consumption, investment, government spending, and net export activity. These summary measures reflect underlying drivers such as employment levels and skills, household savings rates, corporate investment decisions, interest rates, demographics, and government policies.

Richard C. Koo wrote that under ideal conditions, a country's economy should have the household sector as net savers and the corporate sector as net borrowers, with the government budget nearly balanced and net exports near zero. When these relationships become imbalanced, recession can develop within the country or create pressure for recession in another country. Policy responses are often designed to drive the economy back towards this ideal state of balance. A severe (GDP down by 10%) or prolonged (three or four years) recession is referred to as an economic depression, although some argue that their causes and cures can be different. As an informal shorthand, economists sometimes refer to different recession shapes, such as V-shaped, U-shaped, L-shaped and W-shaped recessions.

Main Type of Recession

In fact, Recessions and subsequent growth periods may have distinctive shapes when graphed. In the US, V-shaped, or short-and-sharp contractions followed by rapid and sustained recovery, occurred in 1954 and 1990–91; U-shaped (prolonged slump) in 1974-75, and W-shaped , or double-dip recessions in 1949 and 1980-82. Japan's 1993-94 recession was U-shaped and its 8-out-of-9 quarters of contraction in 1997-99 can be described as L-shaped. Korea, Hong Kong and South-east Asia experienced U-shaped recessions in 1997-98, although Thailand's eight consecutive quarters of decline should be termed L-shaped.

It must be remembered that recessions have

psychological and confidence aspects. For example, if the expectation develops that economic activity will slow, firms may decide to reduce employment levels and save money rather than invest. Such expectations can create a self-reinforcing downward cycle, bringing about or worsening a recession. Consumer confidence is one measure used to evaluate economic sentiment. The term "Animal Spirits" has been used to describe the psychological factors underlying economic activity.

Robert J. Shiller wrote that the term "...refers also to the sense of trust we have in each other, our sense of fairness in economic dealings, and our sense of the extent of corruption and bad faith. When animal spirits are on ebb, consumers do not want to spend and businesses do not want to make capital expenditures or hire people."

1. Balance Sheet Recession: The bursting of a real estate or financial asset price bubble can cause a recession. For example, economist Richard Koo wrote that Japan's "Great Recession" that began in 1990 was a "balance sheet recession." It was triggered by a collapse in land and stock prices, which caused Japanese firms to have negative equity, meaning their assets were worth less than their liabilities.

Despite zero interest rates and expansion of the money supply to encourage borrowing, Japanese corporations in aggregate opted to pay down their debts from their own business earnings rather than borrow to invest as firms typically do. Corporate investment, a key demand component of GDP, fell enormously (22% of GDP) between 1990 and its peak decline in 2003. Japanese firms overall became net savers after 1998, as opposed to borrowers.

Koo argues that it was massive fiscal stimulus (borrowing and spending by the government) that offset this decline and enabled Japan to maintain its level of

GDP. In his view, this avoided a U.S. type Great Depression, in which U.S. GDP fell by 46%. He argued that monetary policy was ineffective because there was limited demand for funds while firms paid down their liabilities. In a balance sheet recession, GDP declines by the amount of debt repayment and un-borrowed individual savings, leaving government stimulus spending as the primary remedy.

2. *Liquidity Trap:* A liquidity trap situation can develop in which interest rates reach near zero (ZIRP) yet do not effectively stimulate the economy. In theory, near-zero interest rates should encourage firms and consumers to borrow and spend. However, if too many individuals or corporations focus on saving or paying down debt rather than spending, lower interest rates have less effect on investment and consumption behavior; the lower interest rates are like "pushing on a string."

Predictors

Although there are no completely reliable predictors, the following are regarded to be possible predictors.

- Inverted yield curve, the model developed by economist Jonathan H. Wright, uses yields on 10-year and three-month Treasury securities as well as the Fed's overnight funds rate. Another model developed by Federal Reserve Bank of New York economists uses only the 10-year/three-month spread. It is, however, not a definite indicator;
- The three-month change in the unemployment rate and initial jobless claims.
- Index of Leading (Economic) Indicators (includes some of the above indicators).
- Lowering of asset prices, such as homes and financial assets, or high personal and corporate debt levels.

Paul Krugman described the U.S. 2009 recession and

Japan's lost decade as liquidity traps. One remedy to a liquidity trap is expanding the money supply via quantitative easing or other techniques in which money is effectively printed to purchase assets, thereby creating inflationary expectations that cause savers to begin spending again. Government stimulus spending and mercantilist policies to stimulate exports and reduce imports are other techniques to stimulate demand. He estimated in March 2010 that developed countries representing 70% of the world's GDP were caught in a liquidity trap.

Coping with Recession

It is pertinent to note that most mainstream economists believe that recessions are caused by inadequate aggregate demand in the economy, and favor the use of expansionary macroeconomic policy during recessions. Strategies favored for moving an economy out of a recession vary depending on which economic school the policymakers follow.

Monetarists would favor the use of expansionary monetary policy, while Keynesian economists may advocate increased government spending to spark economic growth. Supply-side economists may suggest tax cuts to promote business capital investment. When interest rates reach the boundary of an interest rate of zero percent conventional monetary policy can no longer be used and government must use other measures to stimulate recovery.

Keynesians argue that fiscal policy, tax cuts or increased government spending, will work when monetary policy fails. Spending is more effective because of its larger multiplier but tax cuts take effect faster.

Stock Market

Some recessions have been anticipated by stock market declines. In Stocks for the Long Run, Siegel mentions that since 1948, ten recessions were preceded by a stock market decline, by a lead time of 0 to 13 months (average 5.7 months), while ten stock market declines of greater than 10% in the DJIA were not followed by a recession. The real-estate market also usually weakens before a recession. However real-estate declines can last much longer than recessions.

Since the business cycle is very hard to predict, Siegel argues that it is not possible to take advantage of economic cycles for timing investments. Even the National Bureau of Economic Research (NBER) takes a few months to determine if a peak or trough has occurred in the US. During an economic decline, high yield stocks such as fast moving consumer goods, pharmaceuticals, and tobacco tend to hold up better. However when the economy starts to recover and the bottom of the market has passed (sometimes identified on charts as a MACD), growth stocks tend to recover faster. There is significant disagreement about how health care and utilities tend to recover.

Diversifying one's portfolio into international stocks may provide some safety; however, economies that are closely correlated with that of the U.S. may also be affected by a recession in the U.S. There is a view termed the *halfway rule* according to which investors start discounting an economic recovery about halfway through a recession.

In the 16 U.S. recessions since 1919, the average length has been 13 months, although the recent recessions have been shorter. Thus if the 2008 recession followed the average, the downturn in the stock market would have bottomed around November 2008. The actual US stock market bottom of the 2008 recession was in March 2009.

Generally an administration gets credit or blame for the state of economy during its time. This has caused disagreements about when a recession actually started. In an economic cycle, a downturn can be considered a consequence of an expansion reaching an unsustainable state, and is corrected by a brief decline. Thus it is not easy to isolate the causes of specific phases of the cycle. The 1981 recession is thought to have been caused by the tight-money policy adopted by Paul Volcker, chairman of the Federal Reserve Board, before Ronald Reagan took office. Reagan supported that policy.

Walter Heller, chairman of the Council of Economic Advisers in the 1960s, said that "I call it a Reagan-Volcker-Carter recession. The resulting taming of inflation did, however, set the stage for a robust growth period during Reagan's administration."

Notably, economists usually teach that to some degree recession is unavoidable, and its causes are not well understood. Consequently, modern government administrations attempt to take steps, also not agreed upon, to soften a recession.

Effects of Recession

1. Business

Productivity tends to fall in the early stages of a recession, then rises again as weaker firms close. The variation in profitability between firms rises sharply. Recessions have also provided opportunities for anti-competitive mergers, with a negative impact on the wider economy: the suspension of competition policy in the United States in the 1930s may have extended the Great Depression.

2. Unemployment

The full impact of a recession on employment may not be felt for several quarters. Research in Britain shows that low-skilled, low-educated workers and the young are most vulnerable to unemployment in a downturn. After recessions in Britain in the 1980s and 1990s, it took five years for unemployment to fall back to its original levels. Many companies often expect employment discrimination claims to rise during a recession.

3. Social Effects

The living standards of people dependent on wages and salaries are more affected by recessions than those who rely on fixed incomes or welfare benefits. The loss of a job is known to have a negative impact on the stability of families, and individuals' health and well-being.

United Kingdom

The most recent recession to affect the United kingdom was the Late-2000s recession.

United States

According to economists, since 1854, the U.S. has encountered 32 cycles of expansions and contractions, with an average of 17 months of contraction and 38 months of expansion. However, since 1980 there have been only eight periods of negative economic growth over one fiscal quarter or more, and four periods considered recessions:

- July 1981-November 1982: 14 months
- July 1990-March 1991: 8 months
- March 2001-November 2001: 8 months
- December 2007-June 2009: 18 months

Notably, for the past three recessions, the NBER decision has approximately conformed with the definition involving two consecutive quarters of decline. While the 2001 recession did not involve two consecutive quarters of decline, it was preceded by two quarters of alternating decline and weak growth.

Late 2000s

Official economic data shows that a substantial number of nations are in recession as of early 2009. The US entered a recession at the end of 2007, and 2008 saw many other nations follow suit. The US recession of 2007 ended in June, 2009 as the nation entered the current economic recovery.

United States

The United States housing market correction (a possible consequence of United States housing bubble) and subprime mortgage crisis has significantly contributed to a recession.

The 2008/2009 recession is seeing private consumption fall for the first time in nearly 20 years. This indicates the depth and severity of the current recession. With consumer confidence so low, recovery will take a long time. Consumers in the U.S. have been hard hit by the current recession, with the value of their houses dropping and their pension savings decimated on the stock market. Not only have consumers watched their wealth being eroded – they are now fearing for their jobs as unemployment rises.

U.S. employers shed 63,000 jobs in February 2008, the most in five years. Former Federal Reserve chairman Alan Greenspan said on April 6, 2008 that "There is more than a 50 percent chance the United States could go into recession." On October 1, the Bureau of Economic Analysis reported that an additional 156,000 jobs had been lost in September. On April 29, 2008, nine US states were declared by Moody's to be in a recession. In November 2008, employers eliminated 533,000 jobs, the largest single month loss in 34 years. For 2008, an estimated 2.6 million U.S. jobs were eliminated.

The unemployment rate of US grew to 8.5 percent in March 2009, and there were 5.1 million job losses until

March 2009 since the recession began in December 2007. That was about five million more people unemployed compared to just a year prior, which was the largest annual jump in the number of unemployed persons since the 1940s.

Although the US Economy grew in the first quarter by 1%, by June 2008 some analysts stated that due to a protracted credit crisis and "rampant inflation in commodities such as oil, food and steel", the country was nonetheless in a recession. The third quarter of 2008 brought on a GDP retraction of 0.5% the biggest decline since 2001. The 6.4% decline in spending during Q3 on non-durable goods, like clothing and food, was the largest since 1950.

A Nov 17, 2008 report from the Federal Reserve Bank of Philadelphia based on the survey of 51 forecasters, suggested that the recession started in April 2008 and will last 14 months. They project real GDP declining at an annual rate of 2.9% in the fourth quarter and 1.1% in the first quarter of 2009. These forecasts represent significant downward revisions from the forecasts of three months ago.

A December 1, 2008, report from the National Bureau of Economic Research stated that the U.S. has been in a recession since December 2007 (when economic activity peaked), based on a number of measures including job losses, declines in personal income, and declines in real GDP. By July 2009 a growing number of economists believed that the recession may have ended. The National Bureau of Economic Research announced on September 20, 2010 that the 2008/2009 recession ended in June 2009, making it the longest recession since World War II.

Other Countries

In a similar vein few other countries have seen the rate of growth of GDP decrease, generally attributed to reduced liquidity, sector price inflation in food and energy, and the U.S. slowdown. These include the United Kingdom, Ireland, Canada, Japan, China, India, New Zealand and many countries within the EEA. In some, the recession has already been confirmed by experts, while others are still waiting for the fourth quarter GDP growth data to show two consecutive quarters of negative growth. India along with China is experiencing an economic slowdown but not a recession. Also Africa and South Africa are experiencing economic slowdown and global outbreak.

As we have had a glance of recession in this chapter which effects the health of national economies badly, now we will come to issue of unemployment in the next chapter.

REFERENCES

A Estrella, FS Mishkin (1995). *Predicting U.S. Recessions: Financial Variables as Leading Indicators*. MIT Press.

Economic Crisis: When will it End? IBISWorld Recession Briefing Dr. Richard J. Buczynski and Michael Bright, IBISWorld, January 2009

Gaffen, David (2008-11-11). "Recession Puts Halfway Rule to the Test". Online.wsj.com.

Gregory White (2010-04-14). "Presentation by Richard Koo-The Age of Balance Sheet Recessions". Businessinsider.com.

Izzo, Phil (20 September 2010). "Recession Over in June 2009". *The Wall Street Journal*.

Koo, Richard (2009). *The Holy Grail of Macroeconomics-Lessons from Japan's Great Recession*. John Wiley & Sons (Asia) Pte. Ltd..

Krugman, Paul (2009). *The Return of Depression Economics and the Crisis of 2008*. W.W. Norton Company Limited.

Miller, Rich (2008-01-28). "Global Recession Risk Grows as U.S. 'Damage' Spreads". Bloomberg.com.

Robert J. Shiller (2009-06-07). "Why Home Prices May Keep Falling". *New York Times*, June 6, 2009.

Shiller, Robert J. (2009-01-27). "WSJ-Robert Shiller-Animal Spirits Depend on Trust". Online.wsj.com.

Shiskin, Julius (1974-12-01). "The Changing Business Cycle". *New York Times*: p. 222.

Siegel, Jeremy J. (2002). Stocks for the Long Run: The Definitive Guide to Financial Market Returns and Long-Term Investment Strategies, 3rd, New York: McGraw-Hill, 388. ISBN 9780071370486

The Recession that Almost Was. Kenneth Rogoff, International Monetary Fund, Financial Times, April 5, 2002

Vaitilingam, Romesh (17 September 2009). "Recession Britain: New ESRC report on the impact of recession on people's jobs, businesses and daily lives". Economic and *Social Research Council*.

Wright, Jonathan H., The Yield Curve and Predicting Recessions (March 2006). *FEDs Working Paper* No. 2006-7.

7

Unemployment

"They conquer who believe they can. He has not learned the lesson of life who does not each day surmount a fear."

—*Ralph Waldo Emerson*

In the preceding chapter we have put light on the issue of 'recession' which badly affects the economic health of nations in particular and more so globally in general in the present age of globalisation.

Now we come to unemployment problem. The entire analysis is made from the macroeconomic point of view.

A defined by the International Labour Organization (ILO). Unemployment occurs when people are without jobs and they have actively looked for work within the past four weeks. The unemployment rate is a measure of the prevalence of unemployment and it is calculated as a percentage by dividing the number of unemployed individuals by all individuals currently in the labour force.

Economists distinguish between various overlapping types of and theories of unemployment, including cyclical or Keynesian unemployment, frictional unemployment, structural unemployment and classical unemployment. Some additional types of unemployment that are occasionally mentioned are seasonal unemployment, hardcore unemployment, and hidden unemployment. The U.S. BLS measures six types of unemployment, U1-U6.

Though there have been several definitions of voluntary and involuntary unemployment in the economics literature, a simple distinction is often applied. Voluntary unemployment is attributed to the individual's decisions, whereas involuntary unemployment exists because of the socio-economic environment (including the market structure, government intervention, and the level of aggregate demand) in which individuals operate. In these terms, much or most of frictional unemployment is voluntary, since it reflects individual search behavior. Voluntary unemployment includes workers who reject low wage jobs whereas involuntary unemployment includes workers fired due to an economic crisis, industrial decline, company bankruptcy, or organizational restructuring.

On the other hand, cyclical unemployment, structural unemployment, and classical unemployment are largely involuntary in nature. However, the existence of structural unemployment may reflect choices made by the unemployed in the past, while classical (natural) unemployment may result from the legislative and economic choices made by labour unions or political parties. So, in practice, the distinction between voluntary and involuntary unemployment is hard to draw.

The clearest cases of involuntary unemployment are those where there are fewer job vacancies than unemployed workers even when wages are allowed to adjust, so that even if all vacancies were to be filled, some unemployed workers would still remain. This happens with cyclical unemployment, as macroeconomic forces cause microeconomic unemployment which can boomerang back and exacerbate these macroeconomic forces.

There remains considerable theoretical debate regarding the causes, consequences and solutions for unemployment.

Classical, neoclassical and the Austrian School of economics focus on market mechanisms and rely on the invisible hand of the market to resolve unemployment. These theories argue against interventions imposed on the labour market from the outside, such as unionization, minimum wage laws, taxes, and other regulations that they claim discourage the hiring of workers.

Keynesian economics emphasizes the cyclical nature of unemployment and potential interventions to reduce unemployment during recessions. These arguments focus on recurrent supply shocks that suddenly reduce aggregate demand for goods and services and thus reduce demand for workers. Keynesian models recommend government interventions designed to increase demand for workers; these can include financial stimuli, job creation, and expansionist monetary policies.

Marxism focuses on the relations between the controlling owners and the subordinated proletariat whom the owners pit against one another in a constant struggle for jobs and higher wages. This struggle and the unemployment it produces benefit the system by reducing wage costs for the owners. For Marxists the causes of and solutions to unemployment require abolishing capitalism and shifting to socialism or communism.

Besides these three comprehensive theories of unemployment, there are a few types of unemployment that are used to more precisely model the effects of unemployment within the economic system. The main types of unemployment include structural unemployment which focuses on structural problems in the economy and inefficiencies inherent in labour markets including a mismatch between the supply and demand of laborers with necessary skill sets.

Structural arguments emphasize causes and solutions related to disruptive technologies and globalization. Discussions of frictional unemployment focus on voluntary decisions to work based on each individuals' valuation of their own work and how that compares to current wage rates plus the time and effort required to find a job.

Causes and solutions for frictional unemployment often address barriers to entry and wage rates. Behavioral economists highlight individual biases in decision making and often involve problems and solutions concerning sticky wages and efficiency wages.

It is apt to mention that because it has not always been acknowledged or measured systematically, there are limited historical records on unemployment. Industrialization involves economies of scale that often prevent individuals from having the capital to create their own jobs to be self-employed. An individual who cannot either join an enterprise or create a job is unemployed.

As individual farmers, ranchers, spinners, doctors and merchants are organized into large enterprises, those who cannot join or compete become unemployed. Recognition of unemployment occurred slowly as economies across the world industrialized and bureaucratized. The recognition of the concept of "unemployment" is best exemplified through the well documented historical records in England. For example, in 16th century England no distinction was made between vagrants and the jobless; both were simply categorized as "sturdy beggars", to be punished and moved on.

The closing of the monasteries in the 1530s increased

poverty, as the church had helped the poor. In addition, there was a significant rise in enclosure during the Tudor period. Also the population was rising. Those unable to find work had a stark choice: starve or break the law. In 1535, a bill was drawn up calling for the creation of a system of public works to deal with the problem of unemployment, to be funded by a tax on income and capital. A law passed a year later allowed vagabonds to be whipped and hanged. In 1547, a bill was passed that subjected vagrants to some of the more extreme provisions of the criminal law, namely two years servitude and branding with a "V" as the penalty for the first offense and death for the second. During the reign of Henry VIII, as many as 72,000 people are estimated to have been executed. In the 1576 Act each town was required to provide work for the unemployed. The Elizabethan Poor Law of 1601, one of the world's first government-sponsored welfare programs, made a clear distinction between those who were unable to work and those able-bodied people who refused employment.

Under the Poor Law systems of England and Wales, Scotland and Ireland a workhouse was a place where people who were unable to support themselves, could go to live and work. In the early 18th century, there were roughly 10 million people living in England, and an estimated two million were, "vagrants, rogues, prostitutes, beggars or indigents." In 18th century England, half the population was at least occasionally dependent on charity for subsistence. By 1776 some 1,912 parish and corporation workhouses had been established in England and Wales, housing almost 100,000 paupers.

Here it is apt to mention that the decade of the 1930s saw the Great Depression impact unemployment across the globe. One Soviet trading corporation in New York averaged 350 applications a day from Americans seeking jobs in the Soviet Union. In Germany the unemployment rate reached nearly 25% in 1932. In some towns and cities in the north east of England, unemployment reached as high as 70%. Unemployment in Canada reached 27% at the depth of the Depression in 1933. In 1929, the U.S. unemployment rate averaged 3%. In 1933, 25% of all American workers and 37% of all nonfarm workers were unemployed. In Cleveland, Ohio, the unemployment rate was 60%; in Toledo, Ohio, 80%.

There were two million homeless people migrating across the United States. Over 3 million unemployed young men were taken out of the cities and placed into 2600+ work camps managed by the CCC. About 25 million people in the world's 30 richest countries will have lost their jobs between the end of 2007 and the end of 2010 as the economic downturn pushes most countries into recession. In April 2010, the U.S. unemployment rate was 9.9%, but the government's broader U-6 unemployment rate was 17.1%. There are six unemployed people, on average, for each available job. Men account for at least 7 of 10 workers who lost jobs, according to Bureau of Labor Statistics data. The youth unemployment rate was 18.5% in July 2009, the highest July rate since 1948. 34.5% of young African American men were unemployed in October 2009.

Officially, Detroit's unemployment rate is 27%, but the *Detroit News* suggests that nearly half of this city's working-age population may be unemployed. 3.8 million Americans lost their jobs in 2009.

Remarkably, the official unemployment rate in the 16 EU countries that use the euro rose to 10% in December 2009. Latvia had the highest unemployment rate in EU at 22.3% for November 2009. Europe's young workers have been especially hard hit. In November 2009, the unemployment rate in the EU27 for those aged 15–24 was 18.3%. For those under 25, the unemployment rate in Spain was 43.8%.

In fact, a flood of inexpensive consumer goods from China has recently encountered criticism from Europe, the United States and some African countries. In South Africa, some 300,000 textile workers have lost their jobs due to the influx of Chinese goods. The increasing U.S. trade deficit with China has cost 2.4 million American jobs between 2001 and 2008, according to a study by the Economic Policy Institute (EPI). A total of 3.2 million – one in six U.S. factory jobs – have disappeared between 2000 and 2007.

Main Types of Unemployment

1. Classical Unemployment

Classical or real-wage unemployment occurs when real wages for a job are set above the market-clearing level, causing the number of job-seekers to exceed the number of vacancies. Most economists have argued that unemployment increases the more the government intervenes into the economy to try to improve the conditions of those with jobs.

For example, minimum wage laws raise the cost of laborers with few skills to above the market equilibrium, resulting in people who wish to work at the going rate but cannot as wage enforced is greater than their value as workers becoming unemployed.

Laws restricting layoffs made businesses less likely to hire in the first place, as hiring becomes more risky, leaving many young people unemployed and unable to find work. However, this argument is criticized for ignoring numerous external factors and overly simplifying the relationship between wage rates and unemployment- in other words, that other factors may also affect unemployment. Some, such as Murray Rothbard, suggest that even social taboos can prevent wages from falling to the market clearing level.

It is noted that there can be unemployment when job market is in equilibrium. For example, the salary of appliance repairman in a city is $3,000. At this salary, the appliance stores of city want to hire 100 repairmen. But there are 300 repairmen looking for jobs within the city. So there are 200 repairmen looking for jobs are unemployed. At this time, job market is not in equilibrium. But six months later, the salary of appliance repairman in this city drop to $1,000. At this salary, the appliance stores of city want to hire 200 repairmen. There are 200 repairman want to accept jobs. For the rest 100 repairmen, they no longer want to work for this kind of job because the salary is too low.

By this time, job market reaches equilibrium. But there are still 100 repairmen unemployed because they no longer want to work for this kind of job.

2. Cyclical or Keynesian Unemployment

Remarkably, cyclical or Keynesian unemployment, also known as deficient-demand unemployment, occurs when there is not enough aggregate demand in the economy to provide jobs for everyone who wants to work. Demand for most goods and services falls, less production is needed and consequently fewer workers are needed, wages are sticky and do not fall to meet the equilibrium level, and mass unemployment results. Its name is derived from the frequent shifts in the business cycle although unemployment can also be persistent as occurred during the Great Depression of the 1930s.

With cyclical unemployment, the number of unemployed workers exceeds the number of job vacancies, so that even if full employment were attained and all open jobs were filled, some workers would still remain unemployed. Some associate cyclical unemployment with frictional unemployment because the factors that cause the friction are partially due to cyclical variables. For example, a surprise decrease in the money supply may shock rational economic actors and suddenly inhibit aggregate demand.

Basically, classical economists reject the conception of cyclical unemployment and alternatively suggest that the invisible hand of free markets will respond quickly to unemployment and underutilization of resources by a fall in wages followed by a rise in employment. Similarly, Hayek and others from the Austrian school of economics argue that if governments intervene through monetary policy to lower interests rates this will exacerbate unemployment by preventing the market from responding effectively. Keynesian economists on the other hand see the lack of demand for jobs as potentially resolvable by government intervention. One suggested interventions involves deficit spending to boost employment and demand. Another intervention involves an expansionary monetary policy that increases the demand of money which should reduce interest rates which should lead to an increase in non-governmental spending.

3. Marxist Theory

> "It is in the very nature of the capitalist mode of production to overwork some workers while keeping the rest as a reserve army of unemployed paupers."
>
> – *Marx, Theory of Surplus Value,*

Karl Marxis of the opinion that unemployment is inherent within the unstable capitalist system and periodic crises of mass unemployment are to be expected. The function of the proletariat within the capitalist system is to provide a "reserve army of labour" that creates downward pressure on wages. This is accomplished by dividing the proletariat into surplus labour (employees) and under-employment (unemployed). This reserve army of labour fight among themselves for scarce jobs at lower and lower wages. At first glance, unemployment seems inefficient since unemployed workers do not increase profits.

However, unemployment is profitable within the global capitalist system because unemployment lowers wages which are costs from the perspective of the owners. From this perspective low wages benefit the system by reducing economic rents.

Yet, it does not benefit workers. Capitalism unfairly manipulates the market for labour by perpetuating unemployment which lowers laborers' demands for fair wages. Workers are pitted against one another at the service of increasing profits for owners. According to Marx, the only way to permanently eliminate unemployment would be to abolish capitalism and the system of forced competition for wages and then shift to a socialist or communist economic system.

For contemporary Marxists, the existence of persistent unemployment is proof of the inability of capitalism to ensure full employment.

4. Involuntary Unemployment

In *The General Theory*, Keynes argued that neo-classical economic theory did not apply during recessions because of excessive savings and weak private investment in an economy. In consequence, people could be thrown out of work involuntarily and not be able to find acceptable new employment. This conflict between the neoclassical and

Keynesian theories has had strong influence on government policy. The tendency for government is to curtail and eliminate unemployment through increases in benefits and government jobs, and to encourage the job-seeker to both consider new careers and relocation to another city.

In fact, involuntary unemployment does not exist in agrarian societies nor is it formally recognized to exist in underdeveloped but urban societies, such as the mega-cities of Africa and of India/Pakistan. In such societies, a suddenly unemployed person must meet their survival needs either by getting a new job at any price, becoming an entrepreneur, or joining the underground economy of the hustler. Involuntary unemployment is discussed from the narrative standpoint in stories by Ehrenreich, the narrative sociology of Bourdieu, and novels of social suffering such as John Steinbeck's *The Grapes of Wrath.*

5. Full Employment

Basically, in demand-based theory, it is possible to abolish cyclical unemployment by increasing the aggregate demand for products and workers. However, eventually the economy hits an "inflation barrier" imposed by the four other kinds of unemployment to the extent that they exist. Some demand theory economists see the inflation barrier as corresponding to the natural rate of unemployment. The "natural" rate of unemployment is defined as the rate of unemployment that exists when the labour market is in equilibrium and there is pressure for neither rising inflation rates nor falling inflation rates.

An alternative technical term for this rate is the NAIRU or the Non-Accelerating Inflation Rate of Unemployment. No matter what its name, demand theory holds that this means that if the unemployment rate gets "too low," inflation will get worse and worse (accelerate) in the absence of wage and price controls (incomes policies).

It is pertinent to note that one of the major problems with the NAIRU theory is that no one knows exactly what the NAIRU is (while it clearly changes over time). The margin of error can be quite high relative to the actual unemployment rate, making it hard to use the NAIRU in policy-making. Another, normative, definition of full employment might be called the *ideal* unemployment rate. It would exclude all types of unemployment that represent forms of inefficiency. This type of "full employment" unemployment would correspond to only frictional unemployment (excluding that part encouraging the McJobs management strategy) and would thus be very low. However, it would be impossible to attain this full-employment target using only demand-side Keynesian stimulus without getting below the NAIRU and suffering from accelerating inflation (absent incomes policies).

Training programs aimed at fighting structural unemployment would help here. To the extent that hidden unemployment exists, it implies that official unemployment statistics provide a poor guide to what unemployment rate coincides with "full employment" though a utopia.

6. Structural Unemployment

Structural unemployment occurs when a labour market is unable to provide jobs for everyone who wants one because there is a mismatch between the skills of the unemployed workers and the skills needed for the available jobs. Structural unemployment is hard to separate empirically from frictional unemployment, except to say that it lasts longer. As with frictional unemployment, simple demand-side stimulus will not work to easily abolish this type of unemployment.

It is pertinent to note that tructural unemployment may also be encouraged to rise by persistent cyclical unemployment: if an economy suffers from long-lasting low aggregate demand, it means that many of the unemployed become disheartened, while their skills (including job-searching skills) become "rusty" and obsolete.

Problems with debt may lead to homelessness and a fall into the vicious circle of poverty. This means that they may not fit the job vacancies that are created when the economy recovers. Some economists see this scenario as occurring under British Prime Minister Margaret Thatcher during the 1970s and 1980s. The implication is that sustained *high* demand may *lower* structural unemployment. This theory of persistence in structural unemployment has been referred to as an example of path dependence or "hysteresis". Much technological unemployment (e.g. due to the replacement of workers by machines) might be counted as structural unemployment.

Alternatively, technological unemployment might refer to the way in which steady increases in labour productivity mean that fewer workers are needed to produce the same level of output every year. The fact that aggregate demand can be raised to deal with this problem suggests that this problem is instead one of cyclical unemployment.

As indicated by Okun's Law, the demand side must grow sufficiently quickly to absorb not only the growing labour force but also the workers made redundant by increased labour productivity. Otherwise, we see a jobless recovery such as those seen in the United States in both the early 1990s and the early 21st century. Seasonal unemployment may be seen as a kind of structural unemployment, since it is a type of unemployment that is linked to certain kinds of jobs (construction work, migratory farm work). The most-cited official unemployment measures erase this kind of unemployment from the statistics using "seasonal adjustment" techniques.

7. Hidden Unemployment

Hidden, or covered, unemployment is the unemployment of potential workers that is not reflected in official unemployment statistics, due to the way the statistics are collected. In many countries only those who have no work but are actively looking for work (and/or qualifying for social security benefits) are counted as unemployed. Those who have given up looking for work (and sometimes those who are on Government "retraining" programs) are not officially counted among the unemployed, even though they are not employed.

The same applies to those who have taken early retirement to avoid being laid off, but would prefer to be working. The statistic also does not count the "underemployed" - those with part time or seasonal jobs who would rather have full time jobs. In addition, those who are of working age but are currently in full-time education are usually not considered unemployed in government statistics. Because of hidden unemployment, official statistics often underestimate unemployment rates.

8. Frictional Unemployment

Frictional unemployment is the time period between jobs when a worker is searching for, or transitioning from one job to another. It is sometimes called search unemployment and can be voluntary based on the circumstances of the unemployed individual. Frictional unemployment is always present in an economy, so the level of involuntary unemployment is properly the unemployment rate minus the rate of frictional unemployment, which means that increases or decreases in unemployment are normally under-represented in the simple statistics.

Frictional unemployment exists because both jobs and

workers are heterogeneous, and a mismatch can result between the characteristics of supply and demand. Such a mismatch can be related to skills, payment, work-time, location, seasonal industries, attitude, taste, and a multitude of other factors. New entrants (such as graduating students) and re-entrants (such as former homemakers) can also suffer a spell of frictional unemployment. Workers as well as employers accept a certain level of imperfection, risk or compromise, but usually not right away; they will invest some time and effort to find a better match.

This is in fact beneficial to the economy since it results in a better allocation of resources. However, if the search takes too long and mismatches are too frequent, the economy suffers, since some work will not get done. Therefore, governments will seek ways to reduce unnecessary frictional unemployment through multiple means including providing education, advice, training, and assistance such as daycare centers.

The frictions in the labour market are sometimes illustrated graphically with a Beveridge curve, a downward-sloping, convex curve that shows a correlation between the unemployment rate on one axis and the vacancy rate on the other.

Changes in the supply of or demand for labour cause movements along this curve. An increase (decrease) in labour market frictions will shift the curve outwards (inwards).

9. Long-Term Unemployment

Remarkably, this is normally defined, for instance in European Union statistics, as unemployment lasting for longer than one year. It is an important indicator of social exclusion. The Bureau of Labor Statistics reports this as

U4 and U5. The average unemployment duration is significant as well as the average unemployment rate.

The average unemployment rate multilpied by the average unemployment duration represents the degree of the loss of human capital in each country.

Ways to Measure Unemployment

It is pertinent to note that are also different ways national statistical agencies measure unemployment. These differences may limit the validity of international comparisons of unemployment data." To some degree these differences remain despite national statistical agencies increasingly adopting the definition of unemployment by the International Labour Organization.

To facilitate international comparisons, some organizations, such as the OECD, Eurostat, and International Labor Comparisons Program, adjust data on unemployment for comparability across countries.

Though many people care about the number of unemployed individuals, economists typically focus on the unemployment rate. This corrects for the normal increase in the number of people employed due to increases in population and increases in the labour force relative to the population.

The unemployment rate is expressed as a percentage, and is calculated as follows: As defined by the International Labour Organization, "unemployed workers" are those who are currently not working but are willing and able to work for pay, currently available to work, and have actively searched for work. Individuals who are actively seeking job placement must make the effort to: be in contact with an employer, have job interviews, contact job placement agencies, send out resumes, submit applications, respond to advertisements, or some other means of active job searching within the prior four weeks.

Simply looking at advertisements and not responding will not count as actively seeking job placement. Since not all unemployment may be "open" and counted by government agencies, official statistics on unemployment may not be accurate.

Different Methods to Calculate the Unemployment Rate

- *Labour Force Sample Surveys* are the most preferred method of unemployment rate calculation since they give the most comprehensive results and enables calculation of unemployment by different group categories such as race and gender. This method is the most internationally comparable.
- *Official Estimates* are determined by a combination of information from one or more of the other three methods. The use of this method has been declining in favor of Labour Surveys.
- *Social Insurance Statistics* such as unemployment benefits, are computed base on the number of persons insured representing the total labour force and the number of persons who are insured that are collecting benefits. This method has been heavily criticized due to the expiration of benefits before the person finds work.
- *Employment Office Statistics* are the least effective being that they only include a monthly tally of unemployed persons who enter employment offices. This method also includes unemployed who are not unemployed per the ILO definition.

In fact, the primary measure of unemployment, U3, allows for comparisons between countries. Unemployment differs from country to country and across different time periods. For example, during the 1990s and 2000s, the United States had lower unemployment levels than many countries in the European Union, which had significant internal variation, with countries like the UK and Denmark outperforming Italy and France. However, large economic events such as the Great Depression can lead to similar unemployment rates across the globe.

European Union (Eurostat)

Eurostat, the statistical office of the European Union, defines unemployed as those persons age 15 to 74 who are not working, have looked for work in the last four weeks, and ready to start work within two weeks, which conform to ILO standards. Both the actual count and rate of unemployment are reported. Statistical data are available by member state, for the European Union as a whole (EU27) as well as for the euro area (EA16). Eurostat also includes a long-term unemployment rate. This is defined as part of the unemployed who have been unemployed for an excess of 1 year. The main source used is the European Union Labour Force Survey (EU-LFS). The EU-LFS collects data on all member states each quarter.

For monthly calculations, national surveys or national registers from employment offices are used in conjunction with quarterly EU-LFS data. The exact calculation for individual countries, resulting in harmonized monthly data, depend on the availability of the data.

US Bureau of Labor Statistics

The Bureau of Labor Statistics measures employment and unemployment (of those over 15 years of age) using two different labour force surveys conducted by the United States Census Bureau (within the United States Department of Commerce) and/or the Bureau of Labor Statistics (within the United States Department of Labor) that gather employment statistics monthly. The Current Population Survey (CPS), or "Household Survey", conducts a survey based on a sample of 60,000 households. This Survey measures the unemployment rate based on the ILO definition.

The Current Employment Statistics survey (CES), or "Payroll Survey", conducts a survey based on a sample of 160,000 businesses and government agencies that represent 400,000 individual employers. This survey measures only nonagricultural, nonsupervisory employment; thus, it does not calculate an unemployment rate, and it differs from the ILO unemployment rate definition. These two sources have different classification criteria, and usually produce differing results. Additional data are also available from the government, such as the unemployment insurance weekly claims report available from the Office of Workforce Security, within the U.S. Department of Labor Employment & Training Administration. The Bureau of Labor Statistics provides up-to-date numbers via a pdf linked here. The BLS also provides a readable concise current Employment Situation Summary, updated monthly.

The BLS also calculates five alternate measures of unemployment, U1 through U6, that measure different aspects of unemployment:

- U1: Percentage of labour force unemployed 15 weeks or longer.
- U2: Percentage of labour force who lost jobs or completed temporary work.
- U3: Official unemployment rate per the ILO definition occurs when people are without jobs and they have actively looked for work within the past four weeks.
- U4: U3 + "discouraged workers", or those who have stopped looking for work because current economic

conditions make them believe that no work is available for them.

- U5: U4 + other "marginally attached workers", or "loosely attached workers", or those who "would like" and are able to work, but have not looked for work recently.
- U6: U5 + Part time workers who want to work full time, but cannot due to economic reasons (underemployment).

Note: "Marginally attached workers" are added to the total labour force for unemployment rate calculation for U4, U5, and U6. The BLS revised the CPS in 1994 and among the changes the measure representing the official unemployment rate was renamed U3 instead of U5.

Statistics for the U.S. economy as a whole hide variations among groups. For example, in January 2008 U.S. unemployment rates were 4.4% for adult men, 4.2% for adult women, 4.4% for Caucasians, 6.3% for Hispanics or Latinos (all races), 9.2% for African Americans, 3.2% for Asian Americans, and 18.0% for teenagers. Also, the U.S. unemployment rate would be at least 2% higher if prisoners and jail inmates were counted. The unemployment rate is included in a number of major economic indexes including the United States' Conference Board's Index of Leading Indicators a macroeconomic measure of the state of the economy.

Notably, the unemployment rate may be different from the impact of the economy on people. The unemployment figures indicate how many are not working for pay but seeking employment for pay. It is only indirectly connected with the number of people who are actually not working at all or working without pay.

Therefore, critics believe that current methods of measuring unemployment are inaccurate in terms of the impact of unemployment on people as these methods do not take into account the 1.5% of the available working population incarcerated in U.S. prisons (who may or may not be working while incarcerated), those who have lost their jobs and have become discouraged over time from actively looking for work, those who are self-employed or wish to become self-employed, such as tradesmen or building contractors or IT consultants, those who have retired before the official retirement age but would still like to work (involuntary early retirees), those on disability pensions who, while not possessing full health, still wish to work in occupations suitable for their medical conditions, those who work for payment for as little as one hour per week but would like to work full-time.

These people are "involuntary part-time" workers, those who are underemployed, e.g., a computer programmer who is working in a retail store until he can find a permanent job, involuntary stay-at-home mothers who would prefer to work, and graduate and Professional school students who were unable to find worthwhile jobs after they graduated with their Bachelor's degrees. Internationally, some nations' unemployment rates are sometimes muted or appear less severe due to the number of self-employed individuals working in agriculture. Small independent farmers are often considered self-employed; so, they cannot be unemployed.

The impact of this is that in non-industrialized economies, such as the United States and Europe during the early 19th century, overall unemployment was approximately 3% because so many individuals were self-employed, independent farmers; yet, unemployment outside of agriculture was as high as 80%. Many economies industrialize and experience increasing numbers of non-agricultural workers. For example, the United States' non-agricultural labour force increased from 20% in 1800, to 50% in 1850, to 97% in 2000.

The shift away from self-employment increases the percentage of the population who are included in unemployment rates. When comparing unemployment rates between countries or time periods, it is best to consider differences in their levels of industrialization and self-employment. Additionally, the measures of employment and unemployment may be "too high".

In some countries, the availability of unemployment benefits can inflate statistics since they give an incentive to register as unemployed. People who do not really seek work may choose to declare themselves unemployed so as to get benefits; people with undeclared paid occupations may try to get unemployment benefits in addition to the money they earn from their work. However, in countries such as the United States, Canada, Mexico, Australia, Japan and the European Union, unemployment is measured using a sample survey (akin to a Gallup poll).

According to the BLS, a number of Eastern European nations have instituted labour force surveys as well. The sample survey has its own problems because the total number of workers in the economy is calculated based on a sample rather than a census. It is possible to be neither employed nor unemployed by ILO definitions, i.e., to be outside of the "labour force." These are people who have no job and are not looking for one.

Many of these are going to school or are retired. Family responsibilities keep others out of the labour force. Still others have a physical or mental disability which prevents them from participating in labour force activities. And of course some people simply elect not to work, preferring to be dependent on others for sustenance. Typically, employment and the labour force include only work done for monetary gain. Hence, a homemaker is neither part of the labour force nor unemployed. Nor are full-time students nor prisoners considered to be part of the labour force or unemployment.

The latter can be important. In 1999, economists Lawrence F. Katz and Alan B. Krueger estimated that increased incarceration lowered measured unemployment in the United States by 0.17% between 1985 and the late 1990s. In particular, as of 2005, roughly 0.7% of the U.S. population is incarcerated (1.5% of the available working population).

Additionally, children, the elderly, and some individuals with disabilities are typically not counted as part of the labour force in and are correspondingly not included in the unemployment statistics. However, some elderly and many disabled individuals are active in the labour market. In the early stages of an economic boom, unemployment often rises. This is because people join the labour market (give up studying, start a job hunt, etc.) because of the improving job market, but until they have actually found a position they are counted as unemployed.

Similarly, during a recession, the increase in the unemployment rate is moderated by people leaving the labour force or being otherwise discounted from the labour force, such as with the self-employed.

For examples, for the fourth quarter of 2004, according to OECD, (source Employment Outlook 2005 ISBN 92-64-01045-9), normalized unemployment for men aged 25 to 54 was 4.6% in the U.S. and 7.4% in France. At the same time and for the same population the employment rate (number of workers divided by population) was 86.3% in the U.S. and 86.7% in France. This example shows that the unemployment rate is 60% higher in France than in the U.S., yet more people in this demographic are working in France than in the U.S., which is counterintuitive if it is expected that the unemployment rate reflects the health of the labour market.

As such, due to these deficiencies, many labour market economists prefer to look at a range of economic statistics such as labour market participation rate, the percentage of people aged between 15 and 64 who are currently employed or searching for employment, the total number of full-time jobs in an economy, the number of people seeking work as a raw number and not a percentage, and the total number of person-hours worked in a month compared to the total number of person-hours people would like to work. In particular the NBER does not use the unemployment rate but prefer various employment rates to date recessions.

Main Impacts

1. Unemployed individuals are unable to earn money to meet financial obligations. Failure to pay mortgage payments or to pay rent may lead to homelessness through foreclosure or eviction. Across the United States the growing ranks of people made homeless in the foreclosure crisis are generating tent cities. Unemployment increases susceptibility to malnutrition, illness, mental stress, and loss of self-esteem, leading to depression.

According to a study published in Social Indicator Research, even those who tend to be optimistic find it difficult to look on the bright side of things when unemployed. Using interviews and data from German participants aged 16 to 94 – including individuals coping with the stresses of real life and not just a volunteering student population –

the researchers determined that even optimists struggled with being unemployed. Dr. M. Brenner conducted a study in 1979 on the "Influence of the Social Environment on Psychology." Brenner found that for every 10% increase in the number of unemployed there is an increase of 1.2% in total mortality, a 1.7% increase in cardiovascular disease, 1.3% more cirrhosis cases, 1.7% more suicides, 4.0% more arrests, and 0.8% more assaults reported to the police. A more recent study by Christopher Ruhm on the effect of recessions on health found that several measures of health actually improve during recessions. As for the impact of an economic downturn on crime, during the Great Depression the crime rate did not decrease. Because unemployment insurance in the U.S. typically does not replace 50% of the income one received on the job (and one cannot receive it forever), the unemployed often end up tapping welfare programs such as Food Stamps or accumulating debt. Not everyone suffers equally from unemployment. In a prospective study of 9570 individuals over four years, highly conscientiousness people suffered more than twice as much if they became unemployed.

The authors suggested this may be due to conscientious people making different attributions about why they became unemployed, or through experiencing stronger reactions following failure. Some hold that many of the low-income jobs are not really a better option than unemployment with a welfare state (with its unemployment insurance benefits).

But since it is difficult or impossible to get unemployment insurance benefits without having worked in the past, these jobs and unemployment are more complementary than they are substitutes. (These jobs are often held short-term, either by students or by those trying to gain experience; turnover in most low-paying jobs is high.)

Another cost for the unemployed is that the combination of unemployment, lack of financial resources, and social responsibilities may push unemployed workers to take jobs that do not fit their skills or allow them to use their talents. Unemployment can cause underemployment, and fear of job loss can spur psychological anxiety.

2. *Social:* An economy with high unemployment is not using all of the resources, specifically labour, available to it. Since it is operating below its production possibility frontier, it could have higher output if all the workforce were usefully employed. However, there is a trade-off between economic efficiency and unemployment: if the frictionally unemployed accepted the first job they were offered, they would be likely to be operating at below their skill level, reducing the economy's efficiency. During a long period of unemployment, workers can lose their skills, causing a loss of human capital. Being unemployed can also reduce the life expectancy of workers by about 7 years High unemployment can encourage xenophobia and protectionism as workers fear that foreigners are stealing their jobs.

Efforts to preserve existing jobs of domestic and native workers include legal barriers against "outsiders" who want jobs, obstacles to immigration, and/or tariffs and similar trade barriers against foreign competitors. High unemployment can also cause social problems such as crime; if people don't have as much disposable income as before, then it is very likely that crime levels within the economy will increase.

3. *Socio-political:* High levels of unemployment can be causes of civil unrest, in some cases leading to revolution, and particularly totalitarianism. The fall of the Weimar Republic in 1933 and Adolf Hitler's rise to power, which

culminated in World War II and the deaths of tens of millions and the destruction of much of the physical capital of Europe, is attributed to the poor economic conditions in Germany at the time, notably a high unemployment rate of above 20%. Note that the hyperinflation in the Weimar republic is not directly blamed for the Nazi rise – the Inflation in the Weimar Republic occurred primarily in the period 1921–23, which was contemporary with Hitler's Beer Hall Putsch of 1923, and is blamed for damaging the credibility of democratic institutions, but the Nazi party only assumed government in 1933, 10 years after the hyperinflation but in the midst of high unemployment.

Advantages

It must be remembered that unemployment may have advantages as well as disadvantages for the overall economy. Notably, it may help avert inflation, which is argued to have damaging effects, by providing (in Marxian terms) a reserve army of labour, which keeps wages in check. However the direct connection between full local employment and local inflation has been disputed by some due to the recent increase in international trade that supplies low-priced goods even while local employment rates rise to full employment. The inflation-fighting benefits to the *entire economy* arising from a presumed optimum level of unemployment has been studied extensively.

The Shapiro-Stiglitz model suggests that (in the absence of minimum wages) wages are not bid down sufficiently to ever reach 0% unemployment. This occurs because employers know that when wages decrease, workers will shirk and expend less effort. Employers avoid shirking by preventing wages from decreasing so low that workers give up and become unproductive. These higher wages perpetuate unemployment while the threat of unemployment reduces shirking. Before current levels of world trade were developed, unemployment was demonstrated to reduce inflation, following the Phillips curve, or to decelerate inflation, following the NAIRU/natural rate of unemployment theory, since it is relatively easy to seek a new job without losing one's current one.

And when more jobs are available for fewer workers (lower unemployment), it may allow workers to find the jobs that better fit their tastes, talents, and needs. As in the Marxist theory of unemployment, special interests may also benefit: some employers may expect that employees with no fear of losing their jobs will not work as hard, or will demand increased wages and benefit. According to this theory, unemployment may promote general labour productivity and profitability by increasing employers' rationale for their monopsony-like power (and profits). Optimal unemployment has also been defended as an environmental tool to brake the constantly accelerated growth of the GDP to maintain levels sustainable in the context of resource constraints and environmental impacts.

However the tool of denying jobs to willing workers seems a blunt instrument for conserving resources and the environment—it reduces the consumption of the unemployed across the board, and only in the short term. Full employment of the unemployed workforce, all focused toward the goal of developing more environmentally efficient methods for production and consumption might provide a more significant and lasting cumulative environmental benefit and reduced resource consumption.

If so the future economy and workforce would benefit from the resultant structural increases in the sustainable level of GDP growth. Some critics of the "culture of work" such as anarchist Bob Black see employment as overemphasized culturally in modern countries. Such critics often propose quitting jobs when possible, working less, reassessing the cost of living to this end, creation of jobs which are "fun" as opposed to "work," and creating cultural norms where work is seen as unhealthy. These people advocate an "anti-work" ethic for life.

Measures to Control

Generally, societies try a number of different measures to get as many people as possible into work, and various societies have experienced close to full employment for extended periods, particularly during the Post-World War II economic expansion.

The United Kingdom in the 1950s and 60s averaged 1.6% unemployment, while in Australia the 1945 *White Paper on Full Employment in Australia* established a government policy of full employment, which policy lasted until the 1970s when the government ran out of money. However, mainstream economic discussions of full employment since the 1970s suggest that attempts to reduce the level of unemployment below the natural rate of unemployment will fail, resulting only in less output and more inflation.

Demand Side Measures

Notably, many countries aid the unemployed through social welfare programs. These unemployment benefits include unemployment insurance, unemployment compensation, welfare and subsidies to aid in retraining. The main goal of these programs is to alleviate short-term hardships and, more importantly, to allow workers more time to search for a job.

Notably, direct demand-side solution to unemployment is government-funded employment of the able-bodied poor. This was notably implemented in Britain from the 17th century until 1948 in the institution of the workhouse, which provided jobs for the unemployed with harsh conditions and poor wages to dissuade their use. A modern alternative is a job guarantee, where the government guarantees work at a living wage.

United States Families on Relief (in 1,000's)

	1936	*1937*	*1938*	*1939*	*1940*	*1941*
Workers employed						
WPA	1,995	2,227	1,932	2,911	1,971	1,638
CCC and NYA	712	801	643	793	877	919
Other federal work projects	554	663	452	488	468	681
Cases on public assistance						
Social security programs	602	1,306	1,852	2,132	2,308	2,517
General relief	2,946	1,484	1,611	1,647	1,570	1,206
Totals						
Total families helped	5,886	5,660	5,474	6,751	5,860	5,167
Unemployed workers (BLS)	9,030	7,700	10,390	9,480	8,120	5,560
Coverage (cases/ unemployed)	65%	74%	53%	71%	72%	93%

Temporary measures can include public works programs such as the Works Progress Administration. Government-funded employment is not widely advocated as a solution to unemployment, except in times of crisis; this is attributed to the public sector jobs' existence depending directly on the tax receipts from private sector employment.

In the U.S. the unemployment insurance allowance one receives is based solely on previous income (not time worked, family size, etc.) and usually compensates for one-third of one's previous income. To qualify, one must reside in their respective state for at least a year and, of course, work. The system was established by the Social Security Act of 1935.

Although 90% of citizens are covered by unemployment insurance, less than 40% apply for and receive benefits. However, the number applying for and receiving benefits increases during recessions. In cases of highly seasonal industries the system provides income to workers during the off seasons, thus encouraging them to stay attached to the industry. According to classical economic theory, markets reach equilibrium where supply equals demand; everyone who wants to sell at the market price can. Those who do not want to sell at this price do not; in the labour market this is classical unemployment.

Increases in the demand for labour will move the economy along the demand curve, increasing wages and employment. The demand for labour in an economy is derived from the demand for goods and services. As such, if the demand for goods and services in the economy increases, the demand for labour will increase, increasing employment and wages.

Monetary policy and fiscal policy can both be used to increase short-term growth in the economy, increasing the demand for labour and decreasing unemployment.

Supply-Side Measures

The labour market is not 100% efficient: it does not clear, though it may be more efficient than bureaucracy. Some argue that minimum wages and union activity keep wages from falling, which means too many people want to sell their labour at the going price but cannot.

This assumes perfect competition exists in the labour market, specifically that no single entity is large enough to affect wage levels. Advocates of supply-side policies believe those policies can solve this by making the labour market more flexible. These include removing the minimum wage and reducing the power of unions. Supply-siders argue the reforms increase long-term growth. This increased supply of goods and services requires more workers, increasing employment.

It is argued that supply-side policies, which include cutting taxes on businesses and reducing regulation, create jobs and reduce unemployment. Other supply-side policies include education to make workers more attractive to employers. However, recent meta-analyzes involving many studies refute that there is any statistically significant, negative impact of minimum wages on unemployment.

Further, a number of scholars argue that the predicted negative impact is based on incoherent or simplistic logic that ignores mitigating environmental factors, such as non-minimum wage labour markets including farm, service and self employed labourers.

REFERENCES

Arrigo Opocher and Ian Steedman, "Input Price-Input Quantity Relations and the Numeraire", *Cambridge Journal of Economics*, V. 3 (2009): 937-948.

Beckett, Katherine and Bruce Western. (1997) How Unregulated is the U.S. Labor Market?: The Penal System as a Labor Market Institution. Toronto: 1997 American Sociological Association Conference.

Bucholz, R.O. Newton Key, Early modern England, 1485–1714, p. 176 .

Bureau of Labor Statistics, Employment status of the civilian noninstitutional population, 1940 to date. Retrieved March 6, 2009.

Christina Romer (1986). "Spurious Volatility in Historical Unemployment Data", *The Journal of Political Economy*, ***94***(1): 1–37.

Coen, Robert M. (1973). "Labor Force and Unemployment in the 1920's and 1930's: A Re-Examination Based on Postwar Experience", *The Review of Economics and Statistics, 55*(1): 46–55.

Economic Recovery in the Great Depression, Frank G. Steindl, Oklahoma State University.

Garegnani, P. "Heterogeneous Capital, the Production Function and the Theory of Distribution", *Review of Economic Studies*, V. 37, N. 3 (Jul. 1970): 407-436.

Graham White, "The Poverty of Conventional Economic Wisdom and the Search for Alternative Economic and Social Policies", *The Drawing Board: An Australian Review of Public Affairs*, V. 2, N. 2 (Nov. 2001): 67-87.

Growth of China's textile industry slows". Chinadaily.com.cn. March 21, 2007.

Harris, Seymour E. (2005). *The New Economics: Keynes' Influence on Theory and Public Policy*. Kessinger Publishing.

Hayek, Friedrich (1989). *The Collected Works of F.A. Hayek*. University of Chicago Press.

John E. Bregger and Steven E. Haugen (1995). "BLS introduces new range of alternative unemployment measures" Monthly Labor Review, October: 19–29., U.S. Department of Labor, Bureau of Labor Statistics. Retrieved March 6, 2009.

Keynes, John Maynard (2007) [1936]. *The General Theory of Employment, Interest and Money*. Basingstoke, Hampshire: Palgrave Macmillan.

Krueger, Alan B.; Lawrence F. Katz (1999). "New Trend in Unemployment?: The High-Pressure U.S. Labor Market of the 1990s". *Brookings Review*. http://www.brookings.edu/articles/1999/fall_unemployment_katz.aspx. Retrieved 18 February 2011.

Lebergott Stanley (1964). *Manpower in Economic Growth: The American Record since 1800.* New York: McGraw-Hill.

Lebergott Stanley (1964). Manpower in Economic Growth: The American Record since 1800. New York: McGraw-Hill.

Marx, Karl (1863). *Theorien über den Mehrwert (Theory of Surplus Value)*. pp. 478 or at MEW, 26.3, 300. http://www.mlwerke.de/me/me26/me26b471.htm.

Marx, Karl. "The Communist Manifesto". http://www.marxists.org/archive/marx/works/1848/communist-manifesto/index.htm. Retrieved 22 October 2010.

O'Sullivan, Arthur; Steven M. Sheffrin (2003). *Economics: Principles in Action*. Upper Saddle River, New Jersey 07458: Pearson Prentice Hall. pp. 330.

U.S. Department of Labor, Bureau of Labor Statistics, Current Population Survey overview, retrieved May 25, 2007.

Vienneau, Robert L. "On Labour Demand and Equilibria of the Firm", *Manchester School*, V. 73, N. 5 (Sep. 2005): 612-619.

8

Monetary and Fiscal Policy

> "No man will ever be a big executive who feels that he must, either openly or under cover, follow up every order he gives and see that it is done—nor will he ever develop a capable assistant."
>
> —*John Lee Mahin*

Monetary policy and fiscal policy are two important aspects of macroeconomics. Here in this chapter we will put light on these elaborately. The discussion will be supported by facts and examples.

First we come to monetary policy.

Basically, monetary policy is the process by which the monetary authority of a country controls the supply of money, often targeting a rate of interest for the purpose of promoting economic growth and stability. The official goals usually include relatively stable prices and low unemployment.

Monetary theory provides insight into how to craft optimal monetary policy. Monetary policy is referred to as either being expansionary, or a contractionary, where an expansionary policy increases the total supply of money in the economy more rapidly than usual, and a contractionary policy expands the money supply more slowly than usual or even shrinks it.

Expansionary policy is traditionally used to try to combat unemployment in a recession by lowering interest rates in the hope that easy credit will entice businesses into expanding. Contractionary policy is intended to slow inflation in hopes of avoiding the resulting distortions and deterioration of asset values. Monetary policy is contrasted with fiscal policy, which refers to: taxation, government spending, and associated borrowing.

Monetary policy is primarily associated with interest rate and credit. For many centuries there were only two forms of monetary policy: (i) Decisions about coinage; (ii) Decisions to print paper money to create credit. Interest rates, while now thought of as part of monetary authority, were not generally coordinated with the other forms of monetary policy during this time. Monetary policy was seen as an executive decision, and was generally in the hands of the authority with seigniorage, or the power to coin. With the advent of larger trading networks came the ability to set the price between gold and silver, and the price of the local currency to foreign currencies. This official price could be enforced by law, even if it varied from the market price.

Paper money called "jiaozi" originated from promissory notes in 7th century China. Jiaozi did not replace metallic currency, and were used alongside the copper coins. The successive Yuan Dynasty was the first government to use paper currency as the predominant circulating medium. In the later course of the dynasty, facing massive shortages of specie to fund war and their rule in China, they began printing paper money without restrictions, resulting in hyperinflation.

With the creation of the Bank of England in 1694, which acquired the responsibility to print notes and back them with gold, the idea of monetary policy as independent of executive action began to be established. The goal of monetary policy was to maintain the value of the coinage, print notes which would trade at par to specie, and prevent coins from leaving circulation.

The establishment of central banks by industrializing nations was associated then with the desire to maintain the nation's peg to the gold standard, and to trade in a narrow band with other gold-backed currencies. To accomplish this end, central banks as part of the gold standard began setting the interest rates that they charged, both their own borrowers, and other banks who required liquidity. The maintenance of a gold standard required almost monthly adjustments of interest rates.

During the 1870-1920 period, the industrialized nations set up central banking systems, with one of the last being the Federal Reserve in 1913. By this point the role of the central bank as the "lender of last resort" was understood. It was also increasingly understood that interest rates had an effect on the entire economy, in no small part because of the marginal revolution in economics, which demonstrated how people would change a decision based on a change in the economic trade-offs.

It is pertinent to note that monetary policy rests on the relationship between the rates of interest in an economy, that is, the price at which money can be borrowed, and the total supply of money. Monetary policy uses a variety of tools to control one or both of these, to influence outcomes like economic growth, inflation, exchange rates with other currencies and unemployment.

Where currency is under a monopoly of issuance, or where there is a regulated system of issuing currency through banks which are tied to a central bank, the monetary authority has the ability to alter the money supply and thus influence the interest rate (to achieve policy goals).

The beginning of monetary policy as such comes from the late 19th century, where it was used to maintain the gold standard. A policy is referred to as contractionary if it reduces the size of the money supply or increases it only slowly, or if it raises the interest rate. An expansionary policy increases the size of the money supply more rapidly, or decreases the interest rate.

Furthermore, monetary policies are described as follows: accommodative, if the interest rate set by the central monetary authority is intended to create economic growth; neutral, if it is intended neither to create growth nor combat inflation; or tight if intended to reduce inflation. There are several monetary policy tools available to achieve these ends: increasing interest rates by fiat; reducing the monetary base; and increasing reserve requirements. All have the effect of contracting the money supply; and, if reversed, expand the money supply. Since the 1970s, monetary policy has generally been formed separately from fiscal policy.

Even prior to the 1970s, the Bretton Woods system still ensured that most nations would form the two policies separately. Within almost all modern nations, special institutions (such as the Federal Reserve System in the United States, the Bank of England, the European Central Bank, the People's Bank of China, and the Bank of Japan) exist which have the task of executing the monetary policy and often independently of the executive.

In general, these institutions are called central banks and often have other responsibilities such as supervising the smooth operation of the financial system. The primary tool of monetary policy is open market operations. This entails managing the quantity of money in circulation through the buying and selling of various financial instruments, such as treasury bills, company bonds, or foreign currencies.

All of these purchases or sales result in more or less base currency entering or leaving market circulation. Usually, the short term goal of open market operations is to achieve a specific short term interest rate target. In other instances, monetary policy might instead entail the targeting of a specific exchange rate relative to some foreign currency or else relative to gold. For example, in the case of the USA the Federal Reserve targets the federal funds rate, the rate at which member banks lend to one another overnight; however, the monetary policy of China is to target the exchange rate between the Chinese renminbi and a basket of foreign currencies.

In fact, other primary means of conducting monetary policy include:

(i) Discount window lending (lender of last resort);

(ii) Fractional deposit lending (changes in the reserve requirement);

(iii) Moral suasion (cajoling certain market players to achieve specified outcomes);

(iv) "Open mouth operations".

Theory of Monetary Policy

In fact, monetary policy is the process by which the government, central bank, or monetary authority of a country controls (i) the supply of money, (ii) availability of money, and (iii) cost of money or rate of interest to attain a set of objectives oriented towards the growth and stability of the economy. Monetary theory provides insight into how to craft optimal monetary policy.

It is pertinent to note that monetary policy rests on the relationship between the rates of interest in an economy, that is the price at which money can be borrowed, and the total supply of money. Monetary policy uses a variety of tools to control one or both of these, to influence outcomes like economic growth, inflation, exchange rates with other currencies and unemployment.

Where currency is under a monopoly of issuance, or where there is a regulated system of issuing currency through banks which are tied to a central bank, the monetary authority has the ability to alter the money supply and thus influence the interest rate (to achieve policy goals). It is important for policymakers to make credible announcements. If private agents (consumers and firms) believe that policymakers are committed to lowering inflation, they will anticipate future prices to be lower than otherwise (how those expectations are formed is an entirely different matter; compare for instance rational expectations with adaptive expectations).

If an employee expects prices to be high in the future, he or she will draw up a wage contract with a high wage to match these prices. Hence, the expectation of lower wages is reflected in wage-setting behavior between employees and employers (lower wages since prices are expected to be lower) and since wages are in fact lower there is no demand pull inflation because employees are receiving a smaller wage and there is no cost push inflation because employers are paying out less in wages. To achieve this low level of inflation, policymakers must have *credible* announcements; that is, private agents must believe that these announcements will reflect actual future policy.

If an announcement about low-level inflation targets is made but not believed by private agents, wage-setting will anticipate high-level inflation and so wages will be higher and inflation will rise. A high wage will increase a consumer's demand (demand pull inflation) and a firm's costs (cost push inflation), so inflation rises. Hence, if a policymaker's announcements regarding monetary policy are not credible, policy will not have the desired effect. If policymakers believe that private agents anticipate low inflation, they have an incentive to adopt an expansionist monetary policy (where the marginal benefit of increasing economic output outweighs the marginal cost of inflation); however, assuming private agents have rational expectations, they know that policymakers have this incentive. Hence, private agents know that if they anticipate low inflation, an expansionist policy will be adopted that causes a rise in inflation.

Consequently, (unless policymakers can make their announcement of low inflation *credible*), private agents expect high inflation. This anticipation is fulfilled through adaptive expectation (wage-setting behavior);so, there is higher inflation (without the benefit of increased output). Hence, unless credible announcements can be made, expansionary monetary policy will fail. Announcements can be made credible in various ways. One is to establish an independent central bank with low inflation targets (but no output targets).

Hence, private agents know that inflation will be low because it is set by an independent body. Central banks can be given incentives to meet targets (for example, larger budgets, a wage bonus for the head of the bank) to increase their reputation and signal a strong commitment to a policy goal.

Reputation is an important element in monetary policy implementation. But the idea of reputation should not be confused with commitment. While a central bank might have a favorable reputation due to good performance in conducting monetary policy, the same central bank might not have chosen any particular form of commitment (such as targeting a certain range for inflation).

Reputation plays a crucial role in determining how much would markets believe the announcement of a particular commitment to a policy goal but both concepts should not be assimilated. Also, note that under rational expectations, it is not necessary for the policymaker to have established its reputation through past policy actions; as an example, the reputation of the head of the central bank might be derived entirely from his or her ideology, professional background, public statements, etc.

In fact, it has been argued that to prevent some pathologies related to the time inconsistency of monetary policy implementation (in particular excessive inflation), the head of a central bank should have a larger distaste for inflation than the rest of the economy on average. Hence the reputation of a particular central bank is not necessary tied to past performance, but rather to particular institutional arrangements that the markets can use to form inflation expectations. Despite the frequent discussion of credibility as it relates to monetary policy, the exact meaning of credibility is rarely defined.

Such lack of clarity can serve to lead policy away from what is believed to be the most beneficial. For example, capability to serve the public interest is one definition of credibility often associated with central banks. The reliability with which a central bank keeps its promises is also a common definition. While everyone most likely agrees a central bank should not lie to the public, wide disagreement exists on how a central bank can best serve the public interest.

Therefore, lack of definition can lead people to believe they are supporting one particular policy of credibility when they are really supporting another.

Monetarist macroeconomists have sometimes advocated simply increasing the monetary supply at a low, constant rate, as the best way of maintaining low inflation and stable output growth. However, when U.S. Federal Reserve Chairman Paul Volcker tried this policy, starting in October 1979, it was found to be impractical, because of the highly unstable relationship between monetary aggregates and other macroeconomic variables.

Even Milton Friedman acknowledged that money supply targeting was less successful than he had hoped, in an interview with the Financial Times on June 7, 2003. Therefore, monetary decisions today take into account a wider range of factors.

Factors of Decision-Making

- short term interest rates;
- long term interest rates;
- velocity of money through the economy;
- exchange rates;
- credit quality;
- bonds and equities (corporate ownership and debt);
- government versus private sector spending/savings;
- international capital flows of money on large scales;
- financial derivatives such as options, swaps, futures contracts, etc.

In fact, a small but vocal group of people advocate for a return to the gold standard (the elimination of the dollar's fiat currency status and even of the Federal Reserve Bank). Their argument is basically that monetary policy is fraught with risk and these risks will result in drastic harm to the populace should monetary policy fail. Others see another problem with our current monetary policy.

The problem for them is not that our money has nothing physical to define its value, but that fractional reserve lending of that money as a debt to the recipient, rather than a credit, causes all but a small proportion of society (including all governments) to be perpetually in debt. In fact, many economists disagree with returning to a gold standard. They argue that doing so would drastically limit the money supply, and throw away 100 years of advancement in monetary policy. The sometimes complex financial transactions that make big business (especially international business) easier and safer would be much more difficult if not impossible.

Moreover, shifting risk to different people/companies that specialize in monitoring and using risk can turn any financial risk into a known dollar amount and therefore make business predictable and more profitable for everyone involved. Some have claimed that these arguments lost credibility in the global financial crisis of 2008-2009.

Role of Central Banking

It is pertinent to note that central bank influences interest rates by expanding or contracting the monetary base, which consists of currency in circulation and banks' reserves on deposit at the central bank. The primary way that the central bank can affect the monetary base is by open market operations or sales and purchases of second hand government debt, or by changing the reserve requirements. If the central bank wishes to lower interest rates, it purchases government debt, thereby increasing the amount of cash in circulation or crediting banks' reserve accounts. Alternatively, it can lower the interest rate on discounts or overdrafts (loans to banks secured by suitable collateral, specified by the central bank).

If the interest rate on such transactions is sufficiently low, commercial banks can borrow from the central bank to meet reserve requirements and use the additional liquidity to expand their balance sheets, increasing the credit available to the economy. Lowering reserve requirements has a similar effect, freeing up funds for banks to increase loans or buy other profitable assets. A central bank can only operate a truly independent monetary policy when the exchange rate is floating. If the exchange rate is pegged or managed in any way, the central bank will have to purchase or sell foreign exchange. These transactions in foreign exchange will have an effect on the monetary base analogous to open market purchases and sales of government debt; if the central bank buys foreign exchange, the monetary base expands, and vice versa.

But even in the case of a pure floating exchange rate, central banks and monetary authorities can at best "lean against the wind" in a world where capital is mobile. Accordingly, the management of the exchange rate will influence domestic monetary conditions. To maintain its monetary policy target, the central bank will have to sterilize or offset its foreign exchange operations. For example, if a central bank buys foreign exchange (to counteract appreciation of the exchange rate), base money will increase.

Therefore, to sterilize that increase, the central bank must also sell government debt to contract the monetary base by an equal amount. It follows that turbulent activity in foreign exchange markets can cause a central bank to lose control of domestic monetary policy when it is also managing the exchange rate. In the 1980s, many economists began to believe that making a nation's central bank independent of the rest of executive government is the best way to ensure an optimal monetary policy, and those central banks which did not have independence began to gain it. This is to avoid overt manipulation of the tools of monetary policies to effect political goals, such as re-electing the current government. Independence typically means that the members of the committee which conducts monetary policy have long, fixed terms.

Obviously, this is a somewhat limited independence. In the 1990s, central banks began adopting formal, public inflation targets with the goal of making the outcomes, if not the process, of monetary policy more transparent. In other words, a central bank may have an inflation target of 2% for a given year, and if inflation turns out to be 5%, then the central bank will typically have to submit an explanation.

The Bank of England exemplifies both these trends. It became independent of government through the Bank of England Act 1998 and adopted an inflation target of 2.5% RPI (now 2% of CPI). The debate rages on about whether monetary policy can smooth business cycles or not. A central conjecture of Keynesian economics is that the central bank can stimulate aggregate demand in the short run, because a significant number of prices in the economy are fixed in the short run and firms will produce as many goods and services as are demanded (in the long run, however, money is neutral, as in the neoclassical model). There is also the Austrian school of economics, which includes Friedrich von Hayek and Ludwig von Mises's arguments, but most economists fall into either the Keynesian or neoclassical camps on this issue.

Scenario of Developing Countries

Developing countries (DCs) may have problems

establishing an effective operating monetary policy. The primary difficulty is that few developing countries have deep markets in government debt. The matter is further complicated by the difficulties in forecasting money demand and fiscal pressure to levy the inflation tax by expanding the monetary base rapidly. In general, the central banks in many developing countries have poor records in managing monetary policy.

This is often because the monetary authority in a developing country is not independent of government, so good monetary policy takes a backseat to the political desires of the government or are used to pursue other non-monetary goals. For this and other reasons, developing countries that want to establish credible monetary policy may institute a currency board or adopt dollarization.

Such forms of monetary institutions thus essentially tie the hands of the government from interference and, it is hoped, that such policies will import the monetary policy of the anchor nation. Recent attempts at liberalizing and reforming financial markets (particularly the recapitalization of banks and other financial institutions in Nigeria and elsewhere) are gradually providing the latitude required to implement monetary policy frameworks.

Main Types

Basically, in practice, to implement any type of monetary policy the main tool used is modifying the amount of base money in circulation. The monetary authority does this by buying or selling financial assets (usually government obligations). These open market operations change either the amount of money or its liquidity (if less liquid forms of money are bought or sold).

The multiplier effect of fractional reserve banking

amplifies the effects of these actions. Constant market transactions by the monetary authority modify the supply of currency and this impacts other market variables such as short term interest rates and the exchange rate.

In fact, the distinction between the various types of monetary policy lies primarily with the set of instruments and target variables that are used by the monetary authority to achieve their goals. The different types of policy are also called monetary regimes, in parallel to exchange rate regimes.

A fixed exchange rate is also an exchange rate regime; The Gold standard results in a relatively fixed regime towards the currency of other countries on the gold standard and a floating regime towards those that are not. Targeting inflation, the price level or other monetary aggregates implies floating exchange rate unless the management of the relevant foreign currencies is tracking exactly the same variables (such as a harmonized consumer price index).

1. Inflation Targeting: Under this policy approach the target is to keep inflation, under a particular definition such as Consumer Price Index, within a desired range. The inflation target is achieved through periodic adjustments to the Central Bank interest rate target. The interest rate used is generally the interbank rate at which banks lend to each other overnight for cash flow purposes.

Depending on the country this particular interest rate might be called the cash rate or something similar. The interest rate target is maintained for a specific duration using open market operations. Typically the duration that the interest rate target is kept constant will vary between months and years.

This interest rate target is usually reviewed on a monthly

or quarterly basis by a policy committee. Changes to the interest rate target are made in response to various market indicators in an attempt to forecast economic trends and in so doing keep the market on track towards achieving the defined inflation target.

For example, one simple method of inflation targeting called the Taylor rule adjusts the interest rate in response to changes in the inflation rate and the output gap. The rule was proposed by John B. Taylor of Stanford University.

As such inflation targeting approach to monetary policy approach was pioneered in New Zealand. It is currently used in Australia, Brazil, Canada, Chile, Colombia, the Czech Republic, New Zealand, Norway, Iceland, Philippines, Poland, Sweden, South Africa, Turkey, and the United Kingdom.

2. Monetary Aggregates: In the 1980s, several countries used an approach based on a constant growth in the money supply. This approach was refined to include different classes of money and credit (M0, M1 etc.). In the USA this approach to monetary policy was discontinued with the selection of Alan Greenspan as Fed Chairman.

While most monetary policy focuses on a price signal of one form or another, this approach is focused on monetary quantities.

3. Price Level Targeting: Price level targeting is similar to inflation targeting except that CPI growth in one year over or under the long term price level target is offset in subsequent years such that a targeted price-level is reached over time, e.g. five years, giving more certainty about future price increases to consumers. Under inflation targeting what happened in the immediate past years is not taken into account or adjusted for in the current and future years.

*4. **Fixed Exchange Rate:*** This policy is based on maintaining a fixed exchange rate with a foreign currency. There are varying degrees of fixed exchange rates, which can be ranked in relation to how rigid the fixed exchange rate is with the anchor nation. Under a system of fiat fixed rates, the local government or monetary authority declares a fixed exchange rate but does not actively buy or sell currency to maintain the rate.

Instead, the rate is enforced by non-convertibility measures (e.g. capital controls, import/export licenses, etc.). In this case there is a black market exchange rate where the currency trades at its market/unofficial rate. Under a system of fixed-convertibility, currency is bought and sold by the central bank or monetary authority on a daily basis to achieve the target exchange rate.

This target rate may be a fixed level or a fixed band within which the exchange rate may fluctuate until the monetary authority intervenes to buy or sell as necessary to maintain the exchange rate within the band. (In this case, the fixed exchange rate with a fixed level can be seen as a special case of the fixed exchange rate with bands where the bands are set to zero.) Under a system of fixed exchange rates maintained by a currency board every unit of local currency must be backed by a unit of foreign currency (correcting for the exchange rate).

This ensures that the local monetary base does not inflate without being backed by hard currency and eliminates any worries about a run on the local currency by those wishing to convert the local currency to the hard (anchor) currency. Under dollarization, foreign currency (usually the US dollar, hence the term "dollarization") is used freely as the medium of exchange either exclusively or in parallel with local currency.

This outcome can come about because the local population has lost all faith in the local currency, or it may also be a policy of the government (usually to rein in inflation and import credible monetary policy). These policies often abdicate monetary policy to the foreign monetary authority or government as monetary policy in the pegging nation must align with monetary policy in the anchor nation to maintain the exchange rate.

The degree to which local monetary policy becomes dependent on the anchor nation depends on factors such as capital mobility, openness, credit channels and other economic factors.

5. Gold Standard: The gold standard is a system under which the price of the national currency is measured in units of gold bars and is kept constant by the government's promise to buy or sell gold at a fixed price in terms of the base currency. The gold standard might be regarded as a special case of "fixed exchange rate" policy, or as a special type of commodity price level targeting. The minimal gold standard would be a long-term commitment to tighten monetary policy enough to prevent the price of gold from permanently rising above parity.

A full gold standard would be a commitment to sell unlimited amounts of gold at parity and maintain a reserve of gold sufficient to redeem the entire monetary base. Today this type of monetary policy is no longer used by any country, although the gold standard was widely used across the world between the mid-19th century through 1971. Its major advantages were simplicity and transparency.

It is remarkable that the gold standard was abandoned

during the Great Depression, as countries sought to reinvigorate their economies by increasing their money supply. The Bretton Woods system, which was a modified gold standard, replaced it in the aftermath of World War II. However, this system too broke down during the Nixon shock of 1971.

The gold standard induces deflation, as the economy usually grows faster than the supply of gold. When an economy grows faster than its money supply, the same amount of money is used to execute a larger number of transactions. The only way to make this possible is to lower the nominal cost of each transaction, which means that prices of goods and services fall, and each unit of money increases in value. Absent precautionary measures, deflation would tend to increase the ratio of the real value of nominal debts to physical assets over time.

For example, during deflation, nominal debt and the monthly nominal cost of a fixed-rate home mortgage stays the same, even while the dollar value of the house falls, and the value of the dollars required to pay the mortgage goes up. Mainstream economics considers such deflation to be a major disadvantage of the gold standard. Unsustainable (i.e. excessive) deflation can cause problems during recessions and financial crisis lengthening the amount of time a economy spends in recession.

William Jennings Bryan rose to national prominence when he built his historic (though unsuccessful) 1896 presidential campaign around the argument that deflation caused by the gold standard made it harder for everyday citizens to start new businesses, expand their farms, or build new houses.

Policy Adopted by Various Nations

- Australia - Inflation targeting
- Brazil - Inflation targeting
- Canada - Inflation targeting
- Chile - Inflation targeting
- China - Monetary targeting and targets a currency basket
- Czech Republic - Inflation targeting
- Colombia - Inflation targeting
- Hong Kong - Currency board (fixed to US dollar)
- India - Multiple indicator approach
- New Zealand - Inflation targeting
- Norway - Inflation targeting
- Singapore - Exchange rate targeting
- South Africa - Inflation targeting
- Switzerland - Inflation targeting
- Turkey - Inflation targeting
- United Kingdom - Inflation targeting, alongside secondary targets on 'output and employment'.
- United States - Mixed policy (and since the 1980s it is well described by the "Taylor rule," which maintains that the Fed funds rate responds to shocks in inflation and output)

Main Tools

1. Discount Window Lending

Discount window lending is where the commercial banks, and other depository institutions, are able to borrow reserves from the Central Bank at a discount rate. This rate is usually set below short term market rates (T-bills). This enables the institutions to vary credit conditions (i.e., the amount of money they have to loan out), thereby affecting the money supply. It is of note that the Discount Window is the only instrument which the Central Banks do not have total control over. By affecting the money supply, it is theorized, that monetary policy can establish ranges for inflation, unemployment, interest rates, and economic growth.

A stable financial environment is created in which savings and investment can occur, allowing for the growth of the economy as a whole.

2. Monetary Base

Monetary policy can be implemented by changing the size of the monetary base. Central banks use open market operations to change the monetary base. The central bank buys or sells reserve assets (usually financial instruments such as bonds) in exchange for money on deposit at the central bank. Those deposits are convertible to currency. Together such currency and deposits constitute the monetary base which is the general liabilities of the central bank in its own monetary unit. Usually other banks can use base money as a fractional reserve and expand the circulating money supply by a larger amount.

3. Reserve Requirements

The monetary authority exerts regulatory control over banks. Monetary policy can be implemented by changing the proportion of total assets that banks must hold in reserve with the central bank. Banks only maintain a small portion of their assets as cash available for immediate withdrawal; the rest is invested in illiquid assets like mortgages and loans. By changing the proportion of total assets to be held as liquid cash, the Federal Reserve changes the availability of loanable funds. This acts as a change in the money supply. Central banks typically do not change the reserve requirements often because it creates very volatile changes in the money supply due to the lending multiplier.

4. Interest Rates

The contraction of the monetary supply can be achieved *indirectly* by increasing the nominal interest rates. Monetary authorities in different nations have differing levels of control of economy-wide interest rates. In the United States, the Federal Reserve can set the discount rate, as well as achieve the desired Federal funds rate by open market operations. This rate has significant effect on other market interest rates, but there is no perfect relationship. In the United States open market operations are a relatively small part of the total volume in the bond market.

One cannot set independent targets for both the monetary base and the interest rate because they are both modified by a single tool — open market operations; one must choose which one to control. In other nations, the monetary authority may be able to mandate specific interest rates on loans, savings accounts or other financial assets.

By raising the interest rate(s) under its control, a monetary authority can contract the money supply, because higher interest rates encourage savings and discourage borrowing. Both of these effects reduce the size of the money supply.

5. Currency Board

In fact, currency board is a monetary arrangement that pegs the monetary base of one country to another, the anchor nation. As such, it essentially operates as a hard fixed exchange rate, whereby local currency in circulation is backed by foreign currency from the anchor nation at a fixed rate. Thus, to grow the local monetary base an equivalent amount of foreign currency must be held in reserves with the currency board. This limits the possibility for the local monetary authority to inflate or pursue other objectives.

The principal rationales behind a currency board are threefold:

1. To import monetary credibility of the anchor nation;
2. To maintain a fixed exchange rate with the anchor nation;
3. To establish credibility with the exchange rate (the currency board arrangement is the hardest form of fixed exchange rates outside of dollarization).

In theory, it is possible that a country may peg the local currency to more than one foreign currency; although, in practice this has never happened (and it would be a more complicated to run than a simple single-currency currency board). A gold standard is a special case of a currency board where the value of the national currency is linked to the value of gold instead of a foreign currency. The currency board in question will no longer issue fiat money but instead will only issue a set number of units of local currency for each unit of foreign currency it has in its vault.

The surplus on the balance of payments of that country is reflected by higher deposits local banks hold at the central bank as well as (initially) higher deposits of the (net) exporting firms at their local banks. The growth of the domestic money supply can now be coupled to the additional deposits of the banks at the central bank that equals additional hard foreign exchange reserves in the hands of the central bank.

The virtue of this system is that questions of currency stability no longer apply. The drawbacks are that the country no longer has the ability to set monetary policy according to other domestic considerations, and that the fixed exchange rate will, to a large extent, also fix a country's terms of trade, irrespective of economic differences between it and its trading partners.

For example, Hong Kong operates a currency board, as does Bulgaria. Estonia established a currency board pegged to the Deutschmark in 1992 after gaining independence, and this policy is seen as a mainstay of that country's subsequent economic success (see Economy of Estonia for a detailed description of the Estonian currency board).

Argentina abandoned its currency board in January 2002 after a severe recession. This emphasized the fact that currency boards are not irrevocable, and hence may be abandoned in the face of speculation by foreign exchange traders. Following the signing of the Dayton Peace Agreement in 1995, Bosnia and Herzegovina established a currency board pegged to the Deutschmark (since 2002 replaced by the Euro).

It is pertinent to note that currency boards have advantages for *small*, *open* economies that would find independent monetary policy difficult to sustain. They can also form a credible commitment to low inflation.

Other forms of monetary policy, particularly used when interest rates are at or near 0% and there are concerns about deflation or deflation is occurring, are referred to as unconventional monetary policy. These include credit easing, quantitative easing, and signaling. In credit easing, a central bank purchases private sector assets, in order to improve liquidity and improve access to credit. Signaling can be used to lower market expectations for future interest rates. For example, during the credit crisis of 2008, the US Federal Reserve indicated rates would be low for an "extended period", and the Bank of Canada made a "conditional commitment" to keep rates at the lower bound of 25 basis points (0.25%) until the end of the second quarter of 2010.

Having a thorough understanding of monetary policy, now we turn to fiscal policy.

FISCAL POLICY

In common parlance in economics, fiscal policy is the use of government expenditure and revenue collection (taxation) to influence the economy.

Basically, fiscal policy can be contrasted with the other main type of macroeconomic policy, monetary policy, which attempts to stabilize the economy by controlling interest rates and the money supply. The two main instruments of fiscal policy are government expenditure and taxation. Changes in the level and composition of taxation and government spending can impact on the following variables in the economy:

- Aggregate demand and the level of economic activity;
- The pattern of resource allocation;
- The distribution of income.

As such, fiscal policy refers to the use of the government budget to influence the first of these: economic activity.

In fact, the three possible stances of fiscal policy are neutral, expansionary and contractionary. The simplest definitions of these stances are as follows:

- A neutral stance of fiscal policy implies a balanced economy. This results in a large tax. revenue. Government spending is fully funded by tax revenue and overall the budget outcome has a neutral effect on the level of economic activity.

- An expansionary stance of fiscal policy involves government spending exceeding tax revenue.
- A contractionary fiscal policy occurs when government spending is lower than tax revenue.

However, these definitions can be misleading because, even with no changes in spending or tax laws at all, cyclical fluctuations of the economy cause cyclical fluctuations of tax revenues and of some types of government spending, altering the deficit situation; these are not considered to be policy changes.

Therefore, for purposes of the above definitions, "government spending" and "tax revenue" are normally replaced by "cyclically adjusted government spending" and "cyclically adjusted tax revenue". Thus, for example, a government budget that is balanced over the course of the business cycle is considered to represent a neutral fiscal policy stance.

Methods of Funding

In practice, governments spend money on a wide variety of things, from the military and police to services like education and healthcare, as well as transfer payments such as welfare benefits. This expenditure can be funded in a number of different ways:

- Taxation
- Seigniorage, the benefit from printing money
- Borrowing money from the population or from abroad
- Consumption of fiscal reserves.
- Sale of fixed assets (e.g., land).

All of these except taxation are forms of deficit financing.

Borrowing

Remarkably, a fiscal deficit is often funded by issuing bonds, like treasury bills or consols and gilt-edged securities. These pay interest, either for a fixed period or indefinitely. If the interest and capital repayments are too large, a nation may default on its debts, usually to foreign creditors.

Consuming Prior Surpluses

A fiscal surplus is often saved for future use, and may be invested in local (same currency) financial instruments, until needed. When income from taxation or other sources falls, as during an economic slump, reserves allow spending to continue at the same rate, without incurring additional debt.

Economic Effects

Generally, governments use fiscal policy to influence the level of aggregate demand in the economy, in an effort to achieve economic objectives of price stability, full employment, and economic growth. Keynesian economics suggests that increasing government spending and decreasing tax rates are the best ways to stimulate aggregate demand. This can be used in times of recession or low economic activity as an essential tool for building the framework for strong economic growth and working towards full employment.

In theory, the resulting deficits would be paid for by an expanded economy during the boom that would follow; this was the reasoning behind the New Deal. Governments can use a budget surplus to do two things: to slow the pace of strong economic growth, and to stabilize prices when inflation is too high.

Keynesian theory posits that removing spending from the economy will reduce levels of aggregate demand and contract the economy, thus stabilizing prices. Economists debate the effectiveness of fiscal stimulus. The argument mostly centers on crowding out, a phenomenon where government borrowing leads to higher interest rates that offset the stimulative impact of spending.

When the government runs a budget deficit, funds will need to come from public borrowing (the issue of government bonds), overseas borrowing, or monetizing the debt. When governments fund a deficit with the issuing of government bonds, interest rates can increase across the market, because government borrowing creates higher demand for credit in the financial markets.

This causes a lower aggregate demand for goods and services, contrary to the objective of a fiscal stimulus. Neoclassical economists generally emphasize crowding out while Keynesians argue that fiscal policy can still be effective especially in a liquidity trap where, they argue, crowding out is minimal. Some classical and neoclassical economists argue that crowding out completely negates any fiscal stimulus; this is known as the Treasury View, which Keynesian economics rejects.

The Treasury View refers to the theoretical positions of classical economists in the British Treasury, who opposed Keynes' call in the 1930s for fiscal stimulus. The same general argument has been repeated by some neoclassical economists up to the present. In the classical view, the expansionary fiscal policy also decreases net exports, which has a mitigating effect on national output and income. When government borrowing increases interest rates it attracts foreign capital from foreign investors. This is because, all other things being equal, the bonds issued from a country executing expansionary fiscal policy now offer a higher rate of return. In other words, companies wanting to finance projects must compete with their government for capital so they offer higher rates of return. To purchase bonds originating from a certain country, foreign investors must obtain that country's currency.

Therefore, when foreign capital flows into the country undergoing fiscal expansion, demand for that country's currency increases. The increased demand causes that country's currency to appreciate. Once the currency appreciates, goods originating from that country now cost more to foreigners than they did before and foreign goods now cost less than they did before. Consequently, exports decrease and imports increase. Other possible problems with fiscal stimulus include the time lag between the implementation of the policy and detectable effects in the economy, and inflationary effects driven by increased demand. In theory, fiscal stimulus does not cause inflation when it uses resources that would have otherwise been idle.

For instance, if a fiscal stimulus employs a worker who otherwise would have been unemployed, there is no inflationary effect; however, if the stimulus employs a worker who otherwise would have had a job, the stimulus is increasing labor demand while labor supply remains fixed, leading to wage inflation and therefore price inflation.

The concept of a fiscal straitjacket is a general economic principle that suggests strict constraints on government spending and public sector borrowing, to limit or regulate the budget deficit over a time period. The term probably originated from the definition of straitjacket: anything that severely confines, constricts, or hinders. Various states in the United States have various forms of self-imposed fiscal straitjackets.

REFERENCES

Abdel-Monem, Tarik. "What is The Gold Standard?". University of Iowa Center for The Center for International Finance and Development. http://www.uiowa.edu/ifdebook/faq/faq_docs/gold_standard.shtml.

Bernanke, Ben (2006). "Monetary Aggregates and Monetary Policy at the Federal Reserve: A Historical Perspective". Federal Reserve. http://www.federalreserve.gov/newsevents/speech/bernanke20061110a.htm.

Eichengreen, Barry (1992). *Golden Fetters: The Gold Standard and the Great Depression, 1919-1939*. New York: Oxford University Press.

Forder, James (December 2004). ""Credibility" in Context: Do Central Bankers and Economists Interpret the Term Differently?" (pdf). Econ Journals Watch. http://www.econjournalwatch.org/pdf/ForderComment1December2004.pdf.

Friedman, Milton (1960). *A Program for Monetary Stability*. Fordham University Press.

Heyne, P. T., Boettke, P. J., Prychitko, D. L. (2002): The Economic Way of Thinking (10th ed). Prentice Hall.

Larch, M. and J. Nogueira Martins (2009): Fiscal Policy Making in the European Union - An Assessment of Current Practice and Challenges. Routledge.

Nelson, Edward (2007). "Milton Friedman and U.S. Monetary History: 1961-2006". *Federal Reserve Bank of St. Louis Review* (89 (3)): 171. http://research.stlouisfed.org/publications/review/07/05/Nelson.pdf.

Olivei, Giovanni P. (2002). "Switzerland's Approach to Monetary Policy". *New England Economic Review* (Federal Reserve Bank of Boston) (Second Quarter): 57–60. http://www.bos.frb.org/economic/neer/neer2002/neer202l.pdf.

Rogoff, Kenneth, 1985. "The Optimal Commitment to an Intermediate Monetary Target", *Quarterly Journal of Economics* 100, pp. 1169–1189.

Sullivan, arthur; Steven M. Sheffrin (2003). *Economics: Principles in action*. Upper Saddle River, New Jersey 07458: Pearson Prentice Hall. pp. 387.

9

Role of Central Bank

In the preceding chapter, we have presented an elaborate overview of monetary policy and fiscal policy. It is pertinent to note that the notion of central bank plays pivotal role in governance of national economy. In true sense, the central bank is the real custodian of all economic affairs of a nation-state.

Here in this chapter we will elucidate the role of central bank in national economy.

Basically, a central bank, reserve bank, or monetary authority is a public institution that usually issues the currency, regulates the money supply, and controls the interest rates in a country. Central banks often also oversee the commercial banking system within its country's borders. A central bank is distinguished from a normal commercial bank because it has a monopoly on creating the currency of that nation, which is usually that nation's legal tender.

The primary function of a central bank is to provide the nation's money supply, but more active duties include controlling interest rates, and acting as a lender of last resort to the banking sector during times of financial crisis. It may also have supervisory powers, to ensure that banks and other financial institutions do not behave recklessly or fraudulently.

Most developed nations today have an "independent" central bank, that is one which operates under rules designed to prevent political interference. Examples include the European Central Bank (ECB), the Federal Reserve System in the United States and Reserve Bank of India.

Now let us have a look at the evolution of the institution of central bank in historical perspective.

It is pertinent to note that Europe prior to the 17th century most money was commodity money, typically gold or silver. However, promises to pay were widely circulated and accepted as value at least five hundred years earlier in both Europe and Asia. The Song Dynasty was the first to issue generally circulating paper currency, while the Yuan Dynasty was the first to use notes as the predominant circulating medium.

In 1455, in an effort to control inflation, the succeeding Ming Dynasty ended the use of paper money and closed much of Chinese trade. The medieval European Knights Templar ran an early prototype of a central banking system, as their promises to pay were widely respected, and many regard their activities as having laid the basis for the modern banking system. As the first public bank to "offer accounts not directly convertible to coin", the Bank of Amsterdam established in 1609 is considered to be a precursor to a central bank. The central bank of Sweden ("Sveriges Riksbank" or simply "Riksbanken") was founded in Stockholm in 1664, making it the oldest central bank still operating today. This was followed in 1694 by the Bank of England, created by Scottish businessman William Paterson in the City of London at the request of the English government to help pay for a war.

No exaggeration, although central banks today are generally associated with fiat money, the nineteenth and early twentieth centuries central banks in most of Europe and Japan developed under the international gold standard, elsewhere free banking or currency boards were more usual at this time.

Problems with collapses of banks during downturns. however, was leading to wider support for central banks in those nations which did not as yet possess them, most notably in Australia. With the collapse of the gold standard after World War I, central banks became much more widespread. The US Federal Reserve was created by the U.S. Congress through the passing of the Glass-Owen Bill, signed by President Woodrow Wilson on December 23, 1913, whilst Australia established its first central bank in 1920, Colombia in 1923, Mexico and Chile in 1925 and Canada and New Zealand in the aftermath of the Great Depression in 1934. By 1935, the only significant independent nation that did not possess a central bank was Brazil, which developed a precursor thereto in 1945 and created its present central bank twenty years later.

When African and Asian countries gained independence, all of them rapidly established central banks or monetary unions. The People's Bank of China evolved its role as a central bank starting in about 1979 with the introduction of market reforms in that country, and this accelerated in 1989 when the country took a generally capitalist approach to developing at least its export economy. By 2000 the People's Bank of China was in all senses a modern central bank, and emerged as such partly in response to the European Central Bank.

This is the most modern bank model and was introduced with the euro to coordinate the European national banks, which continue to separately manage their respective economies other than currency exchange and base interest rates.

Main Functions and Responsibilities

Notably, functions of a central bank may include:

- implementing monetary policy
- determining Interest rates
- controlling the nation's entire money supply
- the Government's banker and the bankers' bank ("lender of last resort")
- managing the country's foreign exchange and gold reserves and the Government's stock register
- regulating and supervising the banking industry
- setting the official interest rate – used to manage both inflation and the country's exchange rate – and ensuring that this rate takes effect via a variety of policy mechanisms

Monetary Policy

Generally, central banks implement a country's chosen monetary policy. At the most basic level, this involves establishing what form of currency the country may have, whether a fiat currency, gold-backed currency (disallowed for countries with membership of the IMF), currency board or a currency union.

When a country has its own national currency, this involves the issue of some form of standardized currency, which is essentially a form of promissory note: a promise to exchange the note for "money" under certain circumstances. Historically, this was often a promise to exchange the money for precious metals in some fixed amount.

Now, when many currencies are fiat money, the "promise to pay" consists of nothing more than a promise to pay the same sum in the same currency. In many countries, the central bank may use another country's currency either directly (in a currency union), or indirectly, by using a currency board.

In the latter case, local currency is directly backed by the central bank's holdings of a foreign currency in a fixed-ratio; this mechanism is used, notably, in Bulgaria, Hong Kong and Estonia. In countries with fiat money, monetary policy may be used as a shorthand form for the interest rate targets and other active measures undertaken by the monetary authority.

1. Price Stability: In fact, unanticipated inflation leads to lender losses. Nominal contracts attempt to account for inflation. Effort successful if monetary policy able to maintain steady rate of inflation.

2. Economic Growth: Economic growth is enhanced by investment in technological advances in production. Encouragement of savings supplies funds that can be drawn upon for investment.

3. High Employment: The movement of workers between jobs is referred to as frictional unemployment. All unemployment beyond frictional unemployment is classified as unintended unemployment. Reduction in this area is the target of macroeconomic policy.

4. Interest Rate Stability: Volatile interest and exchange rates generate costs to lenders and borrowers. Unexpected changes that cause damage, making policy formulation difficult.

5. Currency issuance: Many central banks are "banks" in the sense that they hold assets (foreign exchange, gold, and other financial assets) and liabilities. A central bank's primary liabilities are the currency outstanding, and these liabilities are backed by the assets the bank owns.

Central banks generally earn money by issuing currency notes and "selling" them to the public for interest-bearing assets, such as government bonds. Since currency usually pays no interest, the difference in interest generates income, called seigniorage. In most central banking systems, this income is remitted to the government. The European Central Bank remits its interest income to its owners, the central banks of the member countries of the European Union. Although central banks generally hold government debt, in some countries the outstanding amount of government debt is smaller than the amount the central bank may wish to hold.

In many countries, central banks may hold significant amounts of foreign currency assets, rather than assets in their own national currency, particularly when the national currency is fixed to other currencies.

6. Conflicts Among Goals: Goals frequently cannot be separated from each other and often conflict. Costs must therefore be carefully weighed before policy implementation.

It must be remembered that there is no standard terminology for the name of a central bank, but many countries use the "Bank of Country" form (e.g., Bank of England, Bank of Canada, Bank of Russia). Some are styled "national" banks, such as the National Bank of Ukraine; but the term "national bank" is more often used by privately-owned commercial banks, especially in the United States. In other cases, central banks may incorporate the word "Central" (e.g. European Central Bank, Central Bank of Ireland). The word "Reserve" is also often included, such as the Reserve Bank of India, Reserve Bank of Australia, Reserve Bank of New Zealand, the South African Reserve Bank, and U.S. Federal Reserve System.

Many countries have state-owned banks or other quasi-government entities that have entirely separate functions, such as financing imports and exports. In some countries, particularly in some Communist countries, the term national bank may be used to indicate both the monetary authority and the leading banking entity, such as the USSR's Gosbank (state bank). In other countries, the term national bank may be used to indicate that the central bank's goals are broader than monetary stability, such as full employment, industrial development, or other goals.

Interest Rate Interventions

Typically a central bank controls certain types of short-term interest rates. These influence the stock- and bond markets as well as mortgage and other interest rates. The European Central Bank for example announces its interest rate at the meeting of its Governing Council; in the case of the Federal Reserve, the Board of Governors. Both the Federal Reserve and the ECB are composed of one or more central bodies that are responsible for the main decisions about interest rates and the size and type of open market operations, and several branches to execute its policies. In the case of the Fed, they are the local Federal Reserve Banks; for the ECB they are the national central banks.

Contrary to popular perception, central banks are not all-powerful and have limited powers to put their policies into effect. Most importantly, although the perception by the public may be that the "central bank" controls some or all interest rates and currency rates, economic theory (and substantial empirical evidence) shows that it is impossible to do both at once in an open economy. Robert Mundell's "impossible trinity" is the most famous formulation of these limited powers, and postulates that it is impossible to target monetary policy (broadly, interest rates), the exchange rate (through a fixed rate) and maintain free capital movement. Since most Western economies are now considered "open" with free capital movement, this essentially means that central banks may target interest rates or exchange rates with credibility, but not both at once. Even when targeting interest rates, most central banks have limited ability to influence the rates actually paid by private individuals and companies.

In the most famous case of policy failure, George Soros arbitraged the pound sterling's relationship to the ECU and (after making $2 billion himself and forcing the UK to spend over $8bn defending the pound) forced it to abandon its policy. Since then he has been a harsh critic of clumsy bank policies and argued that no one should be able to do what he did. The most complex relationships are those between the yuan and the US dollar, and between the euro and its neighbours.

The situation in Cuba is so exceptional as to require the Cuban peso to be dealt with simply as an exception, since the United States forbids direct trade with Cuba. US dollars were ubiquitous in Cuba's economy after its legalization in 1991, but were officially removed from circulation in 2004 and replaced by the convertible peso.

Policy Instruments

The main monetary policy instruments available to central banks are open market operation, bank reserve requirement, interest rate policy, re-lending and re-discount (including using the term repurchase market), and credit policy (often coordinated with trade policy).

While capital adequacy is important, it is defined and regulated by the Bank for International Settlements, and central banks in practice generally do not apply stricter rules. To enable open market operations, a central bank must hold foreign exchange reserves (usually in the form of government bonds) and official gold reserves. It will often have some influence over any official or mandated exchange rates: Some exchange rates are managed, some are market based (free float) and many are somewhere in between ("managed float" or "dirty float").

Interest Rates

By far the most visible and obvious power of many modern central banks is to influence market interest rates; contrary to popular belief, they rarely "set" rates to a fixed number. Although the mechanism differs from country to country, most use a similar mechanism based on a central bank's ability to create as much fiat money as required. The mechanism to move the market towards a 'target rate' (whichever specific rate is used) is generally to lend money or borrow money in theoretically unlimited quantities, until the targeted market rate is sufficiently close to the target. Central banks may do so by lending money to and borrowing money from (taking deposits from) a limited number of qualified banks, or by purchasing and selling bonds.

As an example of how this functions, the Bank of Canada sets a target overnight rate, and a band of plus or minus 0.25%. Qualified banks borrow from each other within this band, but never above or below, because the central bank will always lend to them at the top of the band, and take deposits at the bottom of the band; in principle, the capacity to borrow and lend at the extremes of the band are unlimited.

Other central banks use similar mechanisms. It is also notable that the target rates are generally short-term rates. The actual rate that borrowers and lenders receive on the market will depend on (perceived) credit risk, maturity and other factors.

For example, a central bank might set a target rate for overnight lending of 4.5%, but rates for (equivalent risk) five-year bonds might be 5%, 4.75%, or, in cases of inverted yield curves, even below the short-term rate. Many central banks have one primary "headline" rate that is quoted as the "central bank rate." In practice, they will have other tools and rates that are used, but only one that is rigorously targeted and enforced.

> "The rate at which the central bank lends money can indeed be chosen at will by the central bank; this is the rate that makes the financial headlines." - Henry C.K. Liu. Liu explains further that "the U.S. central-bank lending rate is known as the Fed funds rate. The Fed sets a target for the Fed funds rate, which its Open Market Committee tries to match by lending or borrowing in the money market ... a fiat money system set by command of the central bank. The Fed is the head of the central-bank because the U.S. dollar is the key reserve currency for international trade. The global money market is a USA dollar market. All other currencies markets revolve around the U.S. dollar market."

Accordingly the U.S. situation is not typical of central banks in general. A typical central bank has several interest rates or monetary policy tools it can set to influence markets.

- Marginal lending rate (currently 1.75% in the Eurozone) – a fixed rate for institutions to borrow money from the central bank. (In the USA this is called the discount rate).
- Main refinancing rate (1.00% in the Eurozone) – the publicly visible interest rate the central bank announces. It is also known as *minimum bid rate* and serves as a bidding floor for refinancing loans. (In the USA this is called the federal funds rate).
- Deposit rate (0.25% in the Eurozone) – the rate parties receive for deposits at the central bank.

These rates directly affect the rates in the money market, the market for short term loans.

Open Narket Operations

In fact, through open market operations, a central bank influences the money supply in an economy directly. Each time it buys securities, exchanging money for the security, it raises the money supply. Conversely, selling of securities lowers the money supply. Buying of securities thus amounts to printing new money while lowering supply of the specific security.

The main open market operations are:

- Temporary lending of money for collateral securities ("Reverse Operations" or "repurchase operations", otherwise known as the "repo" market). These operations are carried out on a regular basis, where fixed maturity loans (of 1 week and 1 month for the ECB) are auctioned off.
- Buying or selling securities ("direct operations") on ad-hoc basis.
- Foreign exchange operations such as forex swaps.

Remarkably, all of these interventions can also influence the foreign exchange market and thus the exchange rate. For example the People's Bank of China and the Bank of Japan have on occasion bought several hundred billions of U.S. Treasuries, presumably in order to stop the decline of the U.S. dollar versus the renminbi and the yen.

Capital Requirements

It is apt to mention that all banks are required to hold a certain percentage of their assets as capital, a rate which may be established by the central bank or the banking supervisor. For international banks, including the 55 member central banks of the Bank for International Settlements, the threshold is 8% (see the Basel Capital Accords) of risk-adjusted assets, whereby certain assets (such as government bonds) are considered to have lower risk and are either partially or fully excluded from total assets for the purposes of calculating capital adequacy.

Partly due to concerns about asset inflation and repurchase agreements, capital requirements may be considered more effective than deposit/reserve requirements in preventing indefinite lending: when at the threshold, a bank cannot extend another loan without acquiring further capital on its balance sheet.

Reserve Requirements

In practice, many banks are required to hold a percentage of their deposits as reserves. Such legal reserve requirements were introduced in the nineteenth century to reduce the risk of banks overextending themselves and suffering from bank runs, as this could lead to knock-on effects on other banks.

As the early 20th century gold standard and late 20th century dollar hegemony evolved, and as banks proliferated and engaged in more complex transactions and were able to profit from dealings globally on a moment's notice, these practices became mandatory, if only to ensure that there was some limit on the ballooning of money supply. Such limits have become harder to enforce.

The People's Bank of China retains (and uses) more powers over reserves because the yuan that it manages is a non-convertible currency. Even if reserves were not a legal requirement, prudence would ensure that banks would hold a certain percentage of their assets in the form of cash reserves. It is common to think of commercial banks as passive receivers of deposits from their customers and, for many purposes, this is still an accurate view.

In fact, this passive view of bank activity is misleading when it comes to considering what determines the nation's money supply and credit. Loan activity by banks plays a fundamental role in determining the money supply. The central-bank money after aggregate settlement - final money - can take only one of two forms:

- physical cash, which is rarely used in wholesale financial markets,
- central-bank money.

The currency component of the money supply is far smaller than the deposit component. Currency and bank reserves together make up the monetary base, called M1 and M2.

Exchange Requirements

In fact, to influence the money supply, some central banks may require that some or all foreign exchange receipts (generally from exports) be exchanged for the local currency. The rate that is used to purchase local currency may be market-based or arbitrarily set by the bank. This tool is generally used in countries with non-convertible currencies or partially-convertible currencies.

The recipient of the local currency may be allowed to freely dispose of the funds, required to hold the funds with the central bank for some period of time, or allowed to use the funds subject to certain restrictions.

In other cases, the ability to hold or use the foreign exchange may be otherwise limited. In this method, money supply is increased by the central bank when it purchases the foreign currency by issuing (selling) the local currency.

The central bank may subsequently reduce the money supply by various means, including selling bonds or foreign exchange interventions.

Margin Requirements and Other Tools

In fact, some countries, central banks may have other tools that work indirectly to limit lending practices and otherwise restrict or regulate capital markets. For example, a central bank may regulate margin lending, whereby individuals or companies may borrow against pledged securities. The margin requirement establishes a minimum ratio of the value of the securities to the amount borrowed. Central banks often have requirements for the quality of assets that may be held by financial institutions; these requirements may act as a limit on the amount of risk and leverage created by the financial system. These requirements may be direct, such as requiring certain assets to bear certain minimum credit ratings, or indirect, by the central bank lending to counterparties only when security of a certain quality is pledged as collateral.

For example, the People's Bank of China has been forced into particularly aggressive and differentiating tactics by the extreme complexity and rapid expansion of the economy it manages. It imposed some absolute restrictions on lending to specific industries in 2003, and continues to require between 1% and 3% more reserves from large urban banks (typically focusing on export) than rural ones. This is not by any means an unusual situation.

The USA historically had very wide ranges of reserve requirements between its dozen branches. Domestic development is thought to be optimized mostly by reserve requirements rather than by capital adequacy methods, since they can be more finely tuned and regionally varied.

Banking Supervision and Other Activities

Generally, in some countries a central bank through its subsidiaries controls and monitors the banking sector. In other countries banking supervision is carried out by a government department such as the UK Treasury, or an independent government agency (e.g. UK's Financial Services Authority). It examines the banks' balance sheets and behaviour and policies toward consumers.

Apart from refinancing, it also provides banks with services such as transfer of funds, bank notes and coins or foreign currency. Thus it is often described as the "bank of banks". Many countries such as the United States will monitor and control the banking sector through different agencies and for different purposes, although there is usually significant cooperation between the agencies. For example, money center banks, deposit-taking institutions, and other types of financial institutions may be subject to different (and occasionally overlapping) regulation.

Some types of banking regulation may be delegated to other levels of government, such as state or provincial governments. Any cartel of banks is particularly closely watched and controlled. Most countries control bank mergers and are wary of concentration in this industry due to the danger of groupthink and runaway lending bubbles based on a single point of failure, the credit culture of the few large banks.

Over the past decade, there has been a trend towards increasing the independence of central banks as a way of improving long-term economic performance. However, while a large volume of economic research has been done to define the relationship between central bank independence and economic performance, the results are ambiguous.

Advocates of central bank independence argue that a central bank which is too susceptible to political direction or pressure may encourage economic cycles ("boom and bust"), as politicians may be tempted to boost economic activity in advance of an election, to the detriment of the long-term health of the economy and the country. In this context, independence is usually defined as the central bank's operational and management independence from the government.

The independence of the central bank is enshrined in law. This type of independence is limited in a democratic state; in almost all cases the central bank is accountable at some level to government officials, either through a government minister or directly to a legislature. Even defining degrees of legal independence has proven to be a challenge since legislation typically provides only a framework within which the government and the central bank work out their relationship.

The central bank has the right to set its own policy goals, whether inflation targeting, control of the money supply, or maintaining a fixed exchange rate. While this type of independence is more common, many central banks prefer to announce their policy goals in partnership with the appropriate government departments. This increases the transparency of the policy setting process and thereby increases the credibility of the goals chosen by providing assurance that they will not be changed without notice. In addition, the setting of common goals by the central bank and the government helps to avoid situations where monetary and fiscal policy are in conflict; a policy combination that is clearly sub-optimal.

The central bank has the independence to determine the best way of achieving its policy goals, including the types of instruments used and the timing of their use. This is the most common form of central bank independence. The granting of independence to the Bank of England in 1997 was, in fact, the granting of operational independence; the inflation target continued to be announced in the Chancellor's annual budget speech to Parliament.

The central bank has the authority to run its own operations (appointing staff, setting budgets, etc.) without excessive involvement of the government. The other forms of independence are not possible unless the central bank has a significant degree of management independence. One of the most common statistical indicators used in the literature as a proxy for central bank independence is the "turn-over-rate" of central bank governors.

If a government is in the habit of appointing and replacing the governor frequently, it clearly has the capacity to micro-manage the central bank through its choice of governors. It is argued that an independent central bank can run a more credible monetary policy, making market expectations more responsive to signals from the central bank.

Recently, both the Bank of England (1997) and the European Central Bank have been made independent and follow a set of published inflation targets so that markets know what to expect. Even the People's Bank of China has been accorded great latitude due to the difficulty of problems it faces, though in the People's Republic of China the official role of the bank remains that of a national bank rather than a central bank, underlined by the official refusal to "unpeg" the yuan or to revalue it "under pressure".

The People's Bank of China's independence can thus be read more as independence from the USA which rules the financial markets, than from the Communist Party of China which rules the country. The fact that the Communist Party is not elected also relieves the pressure to please people, increasing its independence. Governments generally have some degree of influence over even "independent" central banks; the aim of independence is primarily to prevent short-term interference. For example, the chairman of the U.S. Federal Reserve Bank is appointed by the

President of the U.S. (all nominees for this post are recommended by the owners of the Federal Reserve, as are all the board members), and his choice must be confirmed by the Congress.

Remarkably, international organizations such as the World Bank, the BIS and the IMF are strong supporters of central bank independence. This results, in part, from a belief in the intrinsic merits of increased independence. The support for independence from the international organizations also derives partly from the connection between increased independence for the central bank and increased transparency in the policy-making process.

The IMF's FSAP review self-assessment, for example, includes a number of questions about central bank independence in the transparency section. An independent central bank will score higher in the review than one that is not independent.

Summing Up

According to the Austrian School, central banking tends to wreak havoc on an economy by systematically devaluing a currency by over creating this currency against nothing of intrinsic value (such as gold), resulting in never-ending inflation. The main opponents to fractional reserve central banking are the proponents of the Austrian business cycle theory, including Ludwig von Mises, Friedrich Hayek and Murray Rothbard, though this economic theory is not generally accepted by mainstream economists.

F.A. Hayek shared a Nobel Prize in economics (with Stockholm school economist, Gunnar Myrdal) in 1974 based on "their pioneering work in the theory of money" among other contributions. Demurrage currencies provide an alternative and perhaps complementary means towards central banking's goal of sustaining economic growth with different specific characteristics and a mechanism that follows naturally from the use of commodity currencies, is more uniform in operation, does not devalue the currency unit, and is more predictable and potentially more decentralized in its operation.

By now you might have come to a perfect understanding of the role of central bank in national economies.

REFERENCES

Quinn, Stephen; Roberds, William (2006), "An Economic Explanation of the Early Bank of Amsterdam, Debasement, Bills of Exchange, and the Emergence of the First Central Bank", Federal Reserve Bank of Atlanta, Working Paper 2006-13

Sullivan, arthur; Steven M. Sheffrin (2003). *Economics: Principles in action*. Upper Saddle River, New Jersey 07458: Pearson Prentice Hall. pp. 254.

Glossary

Absolute advantage: In international trade theory a country which has an absolute advantage in producing a good is able to produce that good more efficiently (more output per unit of input) than any other country.

Accelerator principle: In macroeconomic models the accelerator principle relates changes in the rate of real output growth to the level of desired investment spending (investment demand) in the economy. A decline in the rate of real GDP growth, for example, will cause the amount of investment demand to decrease (the investment demand curve will shift to the left).

Aggregate demand curve: In macroeconomic theory the aggregate demand curve relates the level of real national income (GDP) demanded (the total quantity of goods and services demanded) to the price level (as measured by the GDP deflator).

Aggregate expenditure: In macroeconomic theory aggregate expenditure is the total amount of desired spending by consumers, governments, private investors and foreign buyers (net of spending on imports) at each level of real national income (GDP).

Aggregate supply curve: In macroeconomic theory the short run aggregate supply curve relates the total quantity of goods and services supplied and the price level (as measured by the GDP deflator) *ceteris* *paribus*. The long run aggregate supply curve is a vertical line at the full employment (capacity output) level of real national income (GDP).

Average fixed costs: In the theory of the firm fixed costs are costs of production which are constant whatever the level of output. Average fixed costs are total fixed costs divided by the number of units of output, that is, fixed cost per unit of output.

Average revenue product: In the theory of factor pricing, average revenue product is total revenue divided by the number of units of the factor employed.

Average variable costs: In the theory of the firm, total variable cost divided by the number of units of output.

Balance of payments accounts: A record of all transactions involving a country's exports and imports of goods and services, borrowing and lending.

Balance of trade: A record of a country's exports and imports of goods and services.

Base year: In calculating price indexes, values in the current year are compared to values in some arbitrarily chosen earlier or base year.

Board of directors: Individuals chosen by shareholders in a corporation to administer the affairs of the business.

Capital: Usually used in the "real" sense in economics to refer to machinery and equipment, structures and inventories, that is, produced goods for use in further production. Distinguished from "financial capital", meaning funds which are available to finance the production or acquisition of real capital.

Capital account: That part of the balance of payments

accounts which records a country's lending and borrowing transactions.

Capital consumption allowance: In national income accounting the capital consumption allowance records the amount by which the capital stock has been used up or depreciated during the accounting period. May also be called simply "depreciation."

Capital consumption: The using up of real capital by not maintaining or replacing it as it wears out.

Capital goods: Unlike goods intended to be consumed, capital goods are used to produce other goods. Machinery in a factory would be an example of capital goods.

Capitalism: A system of economic organization characterized by the private ownership of the means of production, private property, and largely market-based control over the production and distribution of goods and services.

Capitalist class: Those members of society who own the capital stock, often used in a pejorative sense by Marxists and other socialist critics of capitalism.

Central bank: An agency empowered by a government to manage a country's monetary and financial institutions, issue and maintain the domestic currency, and handle the official reserves of foreign exchange. Primarily a "bank for banks."

Ceteris paribus: The Latin for "other things being equal."

Change in demand: An increase or decrease in the quantity demanded over a range of prices. Shown by a shift of the demand curve.

Choice: Because wants are unlimited and resources are limited, all economies must choose which goods and services should be produced and in what quantities.

Circular flow: A stylized depiction of the circulation of spending in the economy and the corresponding flows of productive factors and output of produced goods and services.

Classical economics: The economics of Adam Smith, David Ricardo, Thomas Malthus, and later followers such as John Stuart Mill. The theory concentrated on the functioning of a market economy, spelling out a rudimentary explanation of consumer and producer behaviour in particular markets and postulating that in the long term the economy would tend to operate at full employment because increases in supply would create corresponding increases in demand.

Comparative advantage: The ability to produce a tradable good or service at a lower opportunity cost than it could be produced at in another country.

Competition: In the general sense, a contest among sellers or buyers for control over the use of productive resources. Sometimes used as a shorthand way of referring to perfect competition, a market condition in which no individual buyer or seller has any significant influence over price.

Competitive firm: A firm operating under conditions of perfect competition, a market condition in which no individual buyer or seller has any significant influence over price. A competitive firm is a price taker, responding to whatever price is established in the market for its output.

Constant dollars: Sometimes called "real dollars," to refer to price data which have been adjusted to remove the effect of changes in the general level of prices.

Consumer surplus: The net benefit realized by consumers when they are able to buy a good at the prevailing market price. It is equivalent to the difference between the maximum amount consumers would be willing to pay and the amount they actually do pay for the units of the good purchased. Graphically it is the triangle above the market price and below the demand curve.

Consumption function: Generally, the relationship between consumer expenditures and all the influences that determine them. More specifically, the relationship between consumers' disposable incomes (personal income less taxes) and the amount they wish to spend on consumer goods and services.

Consumption spending: Spending on consumer goods and services.

Consumption: Spending to acquire consumer goods and services, or using up those goods and services to satisfy wants.

Coordinates: Intersections of vertical and horizontal values plotted on a graph.

Corporation: A legal entity formed to conduct business and possessing certain privileges not available to single proprietorships or partnerships, notably limited liability which confines the shareholder's possible losses to the amount paid to purchase shares in the business.

Cross-elasticity of demand: The (percentage) change in the quantity demanded of a good consequent upon a (one percent) change in the price of an associated good.

Crowding out: The possible tendency for government spending on goods and services to put upward pressure on interest rates, thereby discouraging private investment spending.

Current account: That part of a country's balance of payments accounts which records the value of goods and services exported minus the value of goods and services imported.

Current dollar: Values which have not been adjusted to remove the influence of changes in the general price level. See "constant dollar."

Cyclical fluctuations: Short term variations in the level of national income such as those which occur from year to year. Contrasted with "secular" changes which occur over longer periods of time.

Deflation: A fall in the general level of all prices. The opposite of inflation.

Depreciation: The using up or wearing out of capital goods.

Deregulation: Reducing or eliminating government intervention to control particular market activities, especially of private firms. For example, removing price controls or monopoly privileges.

Development economics: A sub-discipline within economics specializing in the processes of long term growth and change, especially in the case of the less developed economies.

Diminishing returns: The tendency for additional units of a productive factor to add less and less to total output when combined with other inputs which are to some degree fixed in quantity. Combining more of a variable input, such as labour, with a given amount of some other input, such as capital in the form of a machine, will eventually result in the marginal product for labour declining.

Disposable income: The income a person or household has left to dispose of after income tax has been deducted from personal income. Disposable income may either be spent on consumption or saved.

Dissaving: If individuals or households spend more than their current income they are said to be dissaving.

Economic rent: Any return a factor of production receives in excess of its opportunity cost (what it would have received in its next best use).

Economies of scale: If *all* the inputs in a production process are increased and the output increases by proportionately more than the inputs were increased, economies of scale are being realized. There may also be diseconomies of scale which occur when an increase in all inputs brings about a less than proportionate increase in output.

Elasticity of supply: The (price) elasticity of supply is the percentage change in the quantity supplied of a good or service divided by the percentage change in its (own) price.

Elasticity: When used without a modifier (such as "cross", or "income"), elasticity usually refers to price elasticity which is the percentage change in quantity demanded of a good or service divided by the percentage change in its (own) price.

Entrepreneurship: The ability and willingness to undertake the organization and management of production. As well as making the usual business decisions, entrepreneurship is often associated with the functions of innovating and bearing risks.

Envelope curve: A curve enclosing, by just touching, a number of other curves

Equilibrium condition: A condition which must be

satisfied for equilibrium to exist, equilibrium being defined as a situation in which there is no tendency for change. For example, in the Keynesian expenditure model, the equilibrium condition is that planned spending just equal the current level of national income. Once that condition is satisfied, there is no tendency for the level of national income to change.

Equilibrium price: A price at which the quantity supplied equals the quantity demanded. At this price there is no excess of quantity demanded or supplied, nor is their any deficiency of either and consequently the price will remain at this level.

Equilibrium quantity: The quantity of a good demanded and supplied at the equilibrium price.

Equity: May be used in either of two unrelated senses. In the context of income distribution theory, refers to an objective, goal or principle implying "fairness". In a financial context may refer to a share or portion of ownership.

Excess reserves: The difference between the amount of cash a bank wishes or is required to hold in relation to its deposit liabilities and the amount it actually holds.

Exchange rate: The price of one country's currency in terms of another's.

Explicit cost: The amount spent to obtain or produce something.

Externalities: A benefit or cost associated with an economic transaction which is not taken into account by those directly involved in making it. A beneficial or adverse side effect of production or consumption.

Fiat money: A type of money which has little or no intrinsic value in itself, but which is decreed to be money by the government and is generally accepted in exchange. Modern paper currencies are all fiat money, as are most coins in active circulation.

Firms: Economic entities which buy or employ factors of production and organize them to create goods and services for sale.

Fiscal policy: The use by a government of its expenditures on goods and services and/or tax collections to influence the level of national income.

Fixed capital formation: Investment, the creation of capital goods such as structures, machinery and equipment.

Free rider problem: The undersupplying of a public good caused by the fact that individuals can consume or benefit from the good without paying for it.

Frictional unemployment: Unemployment caused by the loss of jobs due to technological change, the entry of new participants into a labour market, or other normal labour market adjustments.

Functional distribution of income: The division of total income in an economy into shares according to the kind of service provided-usually labour or property (land and capital).

General equilibrium: The condition reached when all markets (for products and productive factors) have cleared, that is, established equilibrium prices and quantities.

Gini coefficient: The ratio of the area between the 45 degree line depicting complete equality and a Lorenz curve to the entire area of the triangle below the 45 degree line.

Government spending: The total outlays by government

on goods and services during some accounting period, usually a year. Government outlays such as welfare benefits to households, for example, are normally excluded from this amount on the grounds that they are merely transfers of income from taxpayers to the beneficiaries of such programs.

Graph: A visual representation of a relationship between two variables, usually drawn to some specified scale.

Gross Domestic Product (GDP): The value of all the goods and services produced in an economy during some accounting period, usually a year.

Gross Domestic Product (GDP) deflator: Nominal GDP divided by real (constant dollar GDP) multiplied by 100. Nominal GDP is the value of output measured in terms of the prices prevailing in the accounting period in question. Real GDP is that output measured in terms of the prices prevailing in some base period. The value of the deflator in the base period is always 100.

Gross investment: Total investment during the accounting period. It includes both additions to the capital stock (net investment) and investment to replace worn out capital (to make up for depreciation).

Gross National Expenditure (GNE): The sum of all spending on consumption and investment plus government spending on goods and services and net exports (total exports minus imports). It is equivalent in value to GDP.

High-powered money: The monetary base, or the total of currency in circulation and commercial bank deposits with the central bank.

Human capital: The stock of knowledge and acquired skills embodied in individuals.

Imperfect competition: A market situation in which one or more buyers or sellers are important enough to have an influence on price.

Income effect: The effect of a change in income on the quantity of a good or service consumed.

Income elasticity of demand: The percentage change in quantity demanded divided by the percentage change in income.

Indifference curve: A curve showing all possible combinations of two goods among which the consumer is indifferent.

Indifference theory: The analysis of consumer demand using indifference curves and an income constraint to demonstrate the reason for the inverse relationship between price and quantity demand. An alternative to the older marginal utility explanation of this phenomenon.

Indirect taxes: Taxes levied on a producer which the producer then passes on to the consumer as part of the price of a good. Distinguished from direct taxes, such as sales taxes which are visible to the person who pays them.

Industry: A group of firms producing similar products. Hence, the auto industry or the steel industry.

Inferior good: A good for which the demand decreases when income increases. When a household's income goes up, it will buy a smaller quantity of such a good.

Inflation: A general rise in the average level of *all* prices.

Interest rate: The percentage rate which must be paid for the use of investable funds.

Interest: The payment made for the use of funds to create capital goods with.

Inventories: Stocks of goods in the hands of producers. These stocks are included in the definition of capital and an increase in inventories is considered to be investment.

Investing: Creating capital goods. Acquiring or producing structures, machinery and equipment or inventories.

Investment spending: The total amount of spending during some period of time on capital goods.

Involuntary unemployment: Unemployment caused by a deficiency in aggregate demand.

Keynesian growth models: Models in which a long run growth path for an economy is traced out by the relations between saving, investing and the level of output.

Keynesian macroeconomics: The theory that shows how a market-based capitalist economy may reach equilibrium with large scale unemployment and how government spending may be used to raise it out of this to a new equilibrium at the full-employment level of output.

Labour: The economically productive capabilities of humans, their physical and mental talents as applied to the production of goods and services.

Laissez-faire: A doctrine advocating a minimum role for government in the economy, such as providing for defence against external enemies, a system of law to protect individuals and their property, and production of such goods and services which for some reason are needed, but would not be produced by private firms.

Land: All natural resources. The "gifts of nature" which are economically useful.

Law of demand: The inverse relationship between price

and quantity of a good or service demanded.

Lender of last resort: The function whereby central banks stand ready to make cash advances to commercial banks in the event they misjudge their cash reserve requirements.

Liabilities: In general, debts owed by individuals or firms. In the case of commercial banks, their liabilities are largely in the form of what they owe their customers, that is, the total amount of deposits held.

Long run average costs: Total costs divided by the number of units of output. The long run average cost curve plots the relationship between output and the lowest possible average total cost when all inputs can be varied.

Long run costs: Production costs when the firm is using its economically most efficient size of plant.

Long run: In the context of the theory of the firm, the long run is a period of time long enough for the firm to vary the quantities of all the inputs it is using, including its physical plant.

Lorenz curve: A curve showing the cumulative percentage of income plotted against the cumulative percentage of population.

Macroeconomics: The branch of economic theory concerned with the economy as a whole. It deals with large aggregates such as total output, rather than with the behaviour of individual consumers and firms.

Majority goods: Goods which are generally available to consumers because they can be mass produced in whatever quantities there is a demand for. Fast food and consumer electronics are good examples.

Marginal analysis: An analytical technique which focuses attention on incremental changes in total values, such as the *last* unit of a good consumed, or the *increase* in total cost.

Marginal benefit: The increase in total benefit consequent upon a one unit increase in the production of a good.

Marginal cost: The increase in total cost consequent upon a one unit increase in the production of a good.

Marginal physical product: The change in total product measured in physical terms caused by a one unit increase in a variable input.

Marginal propensity to consume: The part of the last dollar of disposable income that would be spent on additional consumption.

Marginal propensity to save: The part of the last dollar of disposable income that would be saved.

Marginal revenue: The addition to total revenue resulting from the sale of one additional unit of output.

Marginal revenue product: The change in total revenue that results from employing one more unit of a factor.

Market demand: The relationship between the total quantity of a good demanded and its price.

Market failure: Instances of a free market being unable to achieve an optimum allocation of resources.

Markets: Any coming together of buyers and sellers of produced goods and services or the services of productive factors.

Median voter theorem: The proposition that political parties will tend to adopt moderate policies to appeal to voters near the middle of the political spectrum.

Mercantilism: A body of policy recommendations designed

to promote the development of the early nation states of western Europe in the 17th and 18th centuries. The emphasis was on utilizing trade to increase national wealth at the expense of the countries being traded with through fostering a "favourable balance of trade", by which was meant an excess of exports over imports.

Minority goods: Goods which have a very low elasticity of supply. That is, even large increases in their price can call forth little, if any, additional supply, which means that only the very wealthy can afford them. Large, secluded waterfront properties might be an example.

Monetarism: A view that market economies are inherently self-stabilizing and that variations in the quantity of money are the main cause of fluctuations in the level of aggregate demand.

Monetary base: The same as "high-powered money": cash in commercial banks, plus cash in circulation and deposits of the commercial bank at the central bank.

Monetary policy: The use of the central bank's power to control the domestic money supply to influence the supply of credit, interest rates and ultimately the level of real economic activity.

Money: Anything generally acceptable in exchange. Money serves a number of functions: it is a medium of exchange, it is used as a unit of account, and it can be used as a store of value. In its latter use, it is an alternative to holding value in the form of goods or other types of financial assets such as stocks or bonds.

Monopolistic competition: Essentially the same as imperfect competition: a market situation in which one or more firms may be capable of influencing the price of the product. It is characterized by product differentiation, often established through advertising.

Monopoly: Strictly defined as a market situation in which there is a single supplier of a good or service, but often used to suggest any situation in which a firm has considerable power over market price.

Monopsonistic firm: A firm which is the sole buyer of a good or service, most likely of labour in a particular market.

Multiplier effect: The tendency for a change in aggregate spending to cause a more than proportionate change in the level of real national income.

Mun, Thomas: A British mercantilist writer of the 17th Century.

National income (GDP) deflator: A general way of referring to the price index which measures the average level of the prices of all the goods and services comprising the national income or GDP.

National income: The general term used to refer to the total value of a country's output of goods and services in some accounting period without specifying the formal accounting concept such as Gross Domestic Product.

Natural increase: Growth of the population due to an excess of births over deaths.

Natural monopoly: A market situation in which economies of scale are such that a single firm of efficient size is able to supply the entire market demand.

Natural rate of unemployment: The rate of unemployment that would exist when the economy is operating at full capacity. It would be equal to the amount of frictional unemployment in the system.

Net exports: The total value of goods and services exported during the accounting period minus the total value of goods and services imported.

Net immigration: The total number of people leaving the country to take up permanent residence abroad minus the number of people entering the country for the purpose of taking up permanent residence.

Net investment: Total investment during some accounting period minus the amount of depreciation during the same period.

Normal good: Any good for which the demand increases as incomes increase.

Official settlements account: A record of the net increase or decrease in a country's official foreign exchange reserves.

Open market operations: Central bank purchases or sales of securities in the securities market.

Opportunity cost: The best alternative sacrificed to have or to do something else.

Pareto optimality: The condition which exists when it is impossible to make any individual better off without making any other individual worse off.

Partnership: An unincorporated business owned by two or more people.

Per capita income: Total income divided by the size of the population.

Perfect competition: A market situation in which there are so many sellers (and buyers) that no one seller (or buyer) can exert any influence on the price. All participants in such markets are "price takers".

Personal distribution: The distribution of income on the basis of income groups. For example, by dividing all income recipients into ten groups (deciles) and showing the share each of these groups had of the total income.

Planning curve: The long run average cost curve.

Portfolio theory: The analysis of how an investor can maximize the expected return from a "portfolio" of various kinds of financial assets having given degrees of risk and uncertainty associated with them (or minimize the risk involved in realizing some given expected return).

Positional goods: Goods which are at least in part demanded because their possession or consumption implies social or other status of those acquiring them.

Price discrimination: The selling of a good or service at different prices to different buyers or classes of buyers in the absence of any differences in the costs of supplying it.

Price elasticity of demand: The percentage change in the quantity of a good demanded by the percentage change in its own price.

Price: What must be paid to acquire the right to possess and use a good or service.

Principle of diminishing marginal utility: The proposition that the satisfaction derived from consuming an additional unit of a good or service declines as additional units are acquired.

Principle of Diminishing Returns: The proposition that the marginal product of the last unit of labour employed declines as additional units of labour are employed.

Private goods: A good which cannot be consumed without paying for it and the supply of which is reduced when it is consumed by a particular user of it.

Privatization: The selling-off of publicly owned enterprises to private owners.

Product differentiation: Causing buyers to believe that a particular version of a product is superior to that being offered by competitors.

Production possibilities: Levels of output which are within the range of possibilities for a particular economy.

Production possibility curve: A graphical representation of the boundary between possible and unattainable levels of production in a particular economy.

Profit: When a firm's revenues exceed its costs, profit is the difference between the two.

Public goods: A good which can only be supplied to all if it is supplied to one and the availability of which is not diminished by any one consumer's use of it.

Public interest: The notion that there is some kind of general interest of the community as a whole which can be affected by the actions of governments or private agents.

Quantity theory of money: The idea that there is a direct link between the quantity of money in the economy and the price level.

Quota: A limitation on the amount of a good that can be produced or offered for sale domestically or internationally.

Rational behaviour: Behaviour that is consistent with the attainment of an individual's perception of his or her own best interest.

Real balance effect: The influence a change the quantity of real money has on the quantity of real national income demanded.

Redistribution policy: Measures taken by government to transfer income from some individuals to others.

Relative prices: The relationship between the prices of different goods and services. May be thought of in terms of the amount of one good which can be had for a certain expenditure compared to the amount of another good which can be had for the same expenditure.

Rent-seeking: The activities of individuals or firms to obtain special privileges, such as monopoly power, which will enable them to increase their incomes. Using up resources to win such privileges from governments or their agencies.

Resources: All those things which can be used to produce economic satisfaction.

Risk: Those undertaking investments or the production of goods and services for sale cannot know with certainty whether they will recover the outlays needed to conduct these activities. Although some risks can be insured against (the risk of fire losses for example) there is no way of insuring against the possibility of business losses due to the uncertainty of the market place.

Saving function: The relationship between saving and national income.

Saving: The act of abstaining from consumption. In terms of the national accounts, the difference between personal income less taxes and total consumption spending.

Scarcity: The fact that human wants exceed the means of satisfying them.

Schedule: A table or list of values.

Seasonal unemployment: Unemployment which occurs regularly because of seasonal changes in the demand for certain kinds of labour.

Secular change: Change over a long period of time, such as a decade or more. Distinguished from cyclical change which occurs in shorter time periods such as a year.

Shareholder: Owner of some fraction of the stock issued by a corporation.

Short run: In the theory of the firm, a period of time which is too short for changes to be made in all inputs. For example, a period not long enough to permit the size of the physical plant to be altered.

Simple money multiplier: The amount by which a change in the monetary base is multiplied to bring about the eventual change in the total money supply. It is called the simple money multiplier because it does not take into account possible offsets to the process, such as a rise in the amount of money individuals or households may choose to hold as cash when the money supply increases.

Single proprietorship: A form of unincorporated business in which there is only one owner.

Size distribution of income: The distribution of income among groups of income recipients defined on the basis of the size of their incomes.

Social cost: The real cost to society of having a good or service produced, which may be greater than the private costs incorporated by the producer in its market price.

Social Darwinists: A disparate group of turn-of-the-century commentators on social issues who sought to utilize the Darwinian law of natural selection ("survival of the fittest") as a basis for social policy. The best-known of the social Darwinists was Herbert Spencer.

Stationary state: The economic condition envisioned by the classical writers once the growth of population had reached the point where output per capita was reduced to the subsistence level and the accumulation of capital had reduced the return to investment to zero. The economy would remain in equilibrium with no possibility of future increases in population or per capita incomes.

Substitute goods: Goods which may be used in place of other goods.

Substitution effect: The change in the quantity of a good demanded resulting from a change in its relative price, leaving aside any change in quantity demanded that can be attributable to the associated change in the consumer's real income. It may also be thought of as a a change in the quantity demanded as a result of a movement along a single indifference curve.

Tariff: A tax imposed on an imported good.

Tastes: The preferences of consumers.

Technology: Knowledge which permits or facilitates the transformation of resources into goods and services.

Tort: In law, a private or civil wrong.

Total factor productivity: The growth of real output beyond what can be attributed to increases in the quantities of labour and capital employed.

Transfer payments: Social benefits paid to individuals or households by government.

Unemployment: The non-utilization of labour resources; the condition in which members of the labour force are without jobs. Sometimes used more broadly to refer to the waste of resources when the economy is operating at less than its full potential.

Utilitarian: Refers to a school of philosophy based on the ideas of Jeremy Bentham (1748-1832). The main principle involved was that private morality and government policy should be based on the concept of "general utility,"-the greatest good for the greatest number.

Voluntary export restraint: A restriction placed by an exporting country on the volume of exports it sends to a particular country.

Wages: The general term applied to the earnings of the factor of production, labour.

Wants: The apparently limitless desires or wishes people have for particular goods or services.

X-inefficiency: The failure to minimize costs or maximize returns. (Sometimes referred to as X-efficiency, but carrying the same meaning.)

Bibliography

A Estrella, FS Mishkin (1995). *Predicting U.S. Recessions: Financial Variables as Leading Indicators*. MIT Press.

Abdel-Monem, Tarik. "What is The Gold Standard?". University of Iowa Center for The Center for International Finance and Development. http://www.uiowa.edu/ifdebook/faq/faq_docs/gold_standard.shtml.

Abel, Andrew; Bernanke, Ben (2005). *Macroeconomics* (5th ed.). Pearson

Alan Reynolds (July 1999). "Capital gains tax: Analysis of reform options for Australia" (PDF). Hudson Institute. http://www.asx.com.au/about/pdf/cgt.pdf.

Arrigo Opocher and Ian Steedman (2009). "Input Price-Input Quantity Relations and the Numeraire", *Cambridge Journal of Economics*, V. 3: 937-948.

Atkinson, Robert D. (2006). Supply-side Follies: Why Conservative Economics Fails, Liberal Economics Falters, and Innovation Economics Is the Answer. Lanham: Rowman & Littlefield.

Barro, Robert J. (1989). "New Classicals and Keynesians, or the Good Guys and the Bad Guys". *Swiss Journal of Economics and Statistics* 125 (3): 263–273. http://www.sjes.ch/papers/1989-III-7.pdf

Barro, Robert J. (1997). *Macroeconomics*. Cambridge, Mass: MIT Press. pp. 895.

Bartlett, Bruce (2007-04-06). "How Supply-Side Economics Trickled Down". *New York Times*. http://www.nytimes.com/2007/04/06/opinion/06bartlett.html.

Bartlett, Bruce. "Supply-Side Economics: "Voodoo Economics" or Lasting Contribution?" (PDF). *Laffer Associates* (November 11, 2003). http://web.uconn.edu/cunningham/econ309/lafferpdf.pdf. Retrieved 2008-11-17.

Baumol, William J. and Alan S. Blinder (2006). *Macroeconomics: Principles and Policy*, Tenth edition. Thomson South-Western.

Beaud, Michel; Dostaler, Gilles (1997). *Economic Thought since Keynes*. New York: Routledge.

Beckett, Katherine and Bruce Western. (1997). How Unregulated is the U.S. Labor Market?: The Penal System as a Labor Market Institution. Toronto: 1997 American Sociological Association Conference.

Bernanke, Ben (2006). "Monetary Aggregates and Monetary Policy at the Federal Reserve: A Historical Perspective". Federal Reserve. http://www.federalreserve.gov/newsevents/speech/bernanke20061110a.htm.

Blanchard, Olivier (2000), *Macroeconomics,* Prentice Hall.

Blanchard, Olivier (2000). "What Do We Know About Macroeconomics That Fisher and Wicksell Did Not?". *Quarterly Journal of Economics* 115 (4): 1375-1409.

Blanchard, Olivier (2000). *Macroeconomics* (2nd ed.). Englewood Cliffs, N.J: Prentice Hall.

Blaug, Mark (1986). *Great Economists before Keynes,* Brighton: Wheatsheaf.

Blinder, A. S. (2006). "Can fiscal policy improve macro-stabilization". In Kopcke, E.; Tootell, G. M. B.; Triest, R. K.. *The macroeconomics of fiscal policy*. Cambridge, MA: MIT Press. pp. 23–62.

Blinder, Alan S. (2008). "Keynesian Economics". Concise Encyclopedia of Economics. Library of Economics and Liberty. http://www.econlib.org/library/Enc/KeynesianEconomics.html. Retrieved 25 September 2008.

Block W, Barnett II W. (2007). On Laidler regarding the Austrian business cycle theory. *Review of Austrian Economics*.

Bouchard, Mike (12 Sept 2006). "A Rising Tide Lifts all Boats". townhall.com.

Brownlee, E. (2006). "Fiscal policy in the Reagan administration". In Kopcke, E.; Tootell, G. M. B.; Triest, R. K.. *The macroeconomics of fiscal policy*. Cambr*Italic text*idge, MA: MIT Press. pp. 117–204.

Buchholz, Todd G.; Feldstein, Martin (1999). *New Ideas from Dead Economists: An Introduction to Modern Economic Thought.* New York, New York: Plume.

Bucholz, R.O. Newton Key, Early modern England, 1485–1714, p. 176 .

Burda, Michael C.; Wyplosz, Charles (1997). *Macroeconomics: a European text*. Oxford [Oxfordshire]: Oxford University Press.

Bureau of Labor Statistics, Employment status of the civilian noninstitutional population, 1940 to date. Retrieved March 6, 2009.

Bush, George W. (2007-01-03). "What the Congress Can Do for America". *Wall Street Journal*.

Caballero, Ricardo J. (27 September 2010). "Macroeconomics

after the Crisis: Time to Deal with the Pretense-of-Knowledge Syndrome". MIT Department of Economics Working Paper No. 10-16.

Canto, Victor (1983). "The Foundations of Supply-Side Economics". http://www.highbeam.com/doc/1G1-20004037.html.

Caplan, Bryan (2008-01-02). "What's Wrong With Austrian Business Cycle Theory". Library of Economics and Liberty.

Case, K. E.; Fair, R. C. (2007). *Principles of Economics* (8th ed.). Upper Saddle Rive, NJ: Prentice Hall.

Case, Karl E.; Ray C. Fair (2006). *Principles of Economics.* Englewood Cliffs: Prentice Hall.

Chait, J. (2007). *The Big Con: How Washington Got Hoodwinked and Hijacked by Crackpot Economics.* Boston: Houghton Mifflin.

Christina Romer (1986). "Spurious Volatility in Historical Unemployment Data", *The Journal of Political Economy, 94*(1): 1–37.

Coen, Robert M. (1973). "Labor Force and Unemployment in the 1920's and 1930's: A Re-Examination Based on Postwar Experience", *The Review of Economics and Statistics, 55*(1): 46–55.

Cooley, Thomas F. (1995). *Frontiers of Business Cycle Research.* Princeton: Princeton University Press.

Davidson, Paul (2003). *Financial Markets, Money and the Real World. Aldershot:* Edward Elgar Pub.

Davidson, Paul (2005). "The Post Keynesian school". In Snowdon, Brian; Vane, Howard R. *Modern Macroeconomics.* Cheltenham: E. Elgar. pp. 451-473.

Delong, J. Bradford (2000). "The Triumph of Monetarism?".

The Journal of Economic Perspectives, (American Economic Association) 14 (1): 83-84.

Eichengreen, Barry (1992). *Golden Fetters: The Gold Standard and the Great Depression, 1919-1939.* New York: Oxford University Press.

Farmer, J. Doyne; Foley, Duncan (6 August 2009). Nature. 460. pp. 685-686.

Fengbo Zhang: *Analysis of Chinese Macroeconomy.*

Fletcher, Gordon (2002). "Neoclassical Synthesis". In Snowdon, Brian; Vane, Howard. *An Encyclopedia of Macroeconomics.* Northhampton, Massachusetts: Edward Elgar Publishing. pp. 522-525.

Forder, James (December 2004). ""Credibility" in Context: Do Central Bankers and Economists Interpret the Term Differently?" (pdf). Econ Journals Watch. http://www.econjournalwatch.org/pdf/ForderComment1December2004.pdf.

Friedman, Milton (1960). *A Program for Monetary Stability.* Fordham University Press.

Friedman, Milton. "The 'Plucking Model' of Business Fluctuations Revisited". *Economic Inquiry*: 171–177.

Friedman, Milton. "The Monetary Studies of the National Bureau, 44th Annual Report". *The Optimal Quantity of Money and Other Essays.* Chicago: Aldine. pp. 261–284.

Froyen, Richard (1990). *Macroeconomics, Theories and Policies* (3rd ed.). New York: Macmillan.

Gaffen, David (2008-11-11). "Recession Puts Halfway Rule to the Test". Online.wsj.com.

Galbraith, John Kenneth (1982-02-04). "Recession Economics". *New York Review of Books.*

Gale, W. G. & Orszag, P. R. (2003-05-09). "Bush's Tax Plan Slashes Growth". The Brookings Institution. http:/ /www.brookings.edu/views/op-ed/gale/20030509.htm. Retrieved 2007-10-23.

Gali, Jordi (2008). *Monetary Policy, Inflation, and the Business Cycle.* Princeton: Princeton University Press.

Garegnani, P. "Heterogeneous Capital, the Production Function and the Theory of Distribution", *Review of Economic Studies*, V. 37, N. 3 (Jul. 1970): 407-436.

Garrison, Roger W. (2005). "The Austrian School". In Snowdon, Brian; Vane, Howard R.. *Modern Macroeconomics.* Cheltenham: E. Elgar. pp. 474-516.

Garrison, Roger (1997). In *Business Cycles and Depressions*. David Glasner, ed. New York: Garland Publishing Co., pp. 23-27.

Gärtner, Manfred (2006). *Macroeconomics,* Pearson Education Limited.

Gomes, Joao; Greenwood, Jeremy; Rebelo, Sergio (2001). "Equilibrium Unemployment". *Journal of Monetary Economics* 48 (1): 109–152.

Goodfriend, Marvin; King, Robert G. (1997). "The New Neoclassical Synthesis and the Role of Monetary Policy". *NBER Macroeconomics Annual* 12: 231-283.

Gordon, Tullock (1988). "Why the Austrians are wrong about depressions" (PDF). *The Review of Austrian Economics* 2 (1): 73–78.

Hall, Robert E.; Taylor, John B. (1993). *Macroeconomics*. New York: W.W. Norton. pp. 637.

Hansen, Gary D. (1985). "Indivisible labor and the business cycle". *Journal of Monetary Economics* 16 (3): 309–327.

Harris, Seymour E. (2005). *The New Economics: Keynes' Influence on Theory and Public Policy*. Kessinger Publishing.

Hayek, Friedrich (1989). *The Collected Works of F.A. Hayek*. University of Chicago Press.

Heijdra, B.J.; Ploeg, F. van der (2002). *Foundations of Modern Macroeconomics,* Oxford University Press.

Heyne, P. T., Boettke, P. J., Prychitko, D. L. (2002). *The Economic Way of Thinking* (10th ed). Prentice Hall.

Hoover, Kevin (2008). "New Classical Macroeconomics". The Concise Encyclopedia of Economics. Library of Economics and Liberty. http://www.econlib.org/library/Enc/NewClassicalMacroeconomics.html. Retrieved 13 July 2010.

Howitt, Peter (2002). Snowdon, Brian; Vane, Howard. eds. *An Encyclopedia of Macroeconomics*. Cheltenham: Edward Elgar Publishing.

Izzo, Phil (20 September 2010). "Recession Over in June 2009". *The Wall Street Journal*.

John E. Bregger and Steven E. Haugen (1995). "BLS introduces new range of alternative unemployment measures" Monthly Labor Review, October: 19–29., U.S. Department of Labor, Bureau of Labor Statistics. Retrieved March 6, 2009.

Keeler, JP. (2001). Empirical Evidence on the Austrian Business Cycle Theory. *Review of Austrian Economics* 14 (4).

Keynes, John Maynard (2007). *The General Theory of Employment, Interest and Money*. Basingstoke, Hampshire: Palgrave Macmillan.

Kirman, Alan P. (1992). "Whom or What does the Representative Individual Represent?". *Journal of Economic Perspectives* 6 (2): 117–136.

Kocherlakota, Narayana R. (May 2010). "Modern macroeconomic models as tools for economic policy". The Region. Federal Reserve Bank of Minneapolis.

Koo, Richard (2009). *The Holy Grail of Macroeconomics-Lessons from Japan's Great Recession*. John Wiley & Sons (Asia) Pte. Ltd..

Krueger, Alan B.; Lawrence F. Katz (1999). "New Trend in Unemployment?: The High-Pressure U.S. Labor Market of the 1990s". *Brookings Review*. http://www.brookings.edu/articles/1999/fall_unemployment_katz.aspx. Retrieved 18 February 2011.

Krugman, Paul (1998-12-04). "The Hangover Theory". Slate. http://www.slate.com/id/9593. Retrieved 2008-06-20.

Krugman, Paul (2 September 2009). "How Did Economists Get It So Wrong?". The Concise Encyclopedia of Economics. The New York Times. http://www.nytimes.com/2009/09/06/magazine/06Economic-t.html. Retrieved 16 February 2011.

Krugman, Paul (2009). *The Return of Depression Economics and the Crisis of 2008*. W.W. Norton Company Limited.

Krugman, Paul; Wells, Robin (2009). *Economics*. New York: Worth Publishers.

Kydland, Finn E.; Prescott, Edward C. (1982). "Time to Build and Aggregate Fluctuations". *Econometrica* 50 (6): 1345–1370.

Laider, D. (1999). *Fabricating the Keynesian Revolution*. Cambridge University Press. Preview.

Larch, M. and J. Nogueira Martins (2009): Fiscal Policy Making in the European Union - An Assessment of Current Practice and Challenges. Routledge.

Lebergott Stanley (1964). *Manpower in Economic Growth: The American Record since 1800*. New York: McGraw-Hill.

Leonardo Auernheimer, "The Honest Government's Guide to the Revenue From the Creation of Money," Journal of Political Economy, Vol. 82, No. 3, May/June 1974, pp. 598-606.

Long, John B., Jr.; Plosser, Charles (1983). "Real Business Cycles". *Journal of Political Economy* 91 (1): 39–69.

Lucas, Robert E., Jr. (1977). "Understanding Business Cycles". *Carnegie-Rochester Conference Series on Public Policy* 5: 7–29.

Malabre, Jr., Alfred L. (1994). *Lost Prophets: An Insider's History of the Modern Economists*, p. 182. Harvard Business School Press.

Mankiw, N. Gregory (2002). *Macroeconomics* (5th ed.). Worth

Mankiw, N. Gregory (December 1990). "A Quick Referesher Course in Macroeconomics". *Journal of Economic Literature* 28 (4): 1645-1660.

Mark, Nelson Chung (2001). *International macroeconomics and finance: theory and econometric methods*. Oxford: Cambridge.

Martin, Douglas (2005-08-31). "Jude Wanniski, 69, Journalist Who Coined the Term 'Supply-Side Economics,' Dies". *New York Times*. http://www.nytimes.com/2005/08/31/business/31wanniski.html.

Martin, Keith D. (2010). *A Liberal Mandate: Reflections on our Founding Vision and Rants on how we have Failed to Achieve it*. Silver Spring, MD: WeitPress.

Marx, Karl (1863). *Theorien über den Mehrwert (Theory of Surplus Value)*. pp. 478 or at MEW, 26.3, 300. http:/ /www.mlwerke.de/me/me26/me26b471.htm.

Mayer, Thomas (Winter 1998). "Boettke's Austrian critique of mainstream economics: An empiricist's response". *Critical Review* (Routledge): 151–171.

McCallum, Bennett T. (2008). "Monetarism". *The Concise Encyclopedia of Economics.* Library of Economics and Liberty. http://www.econlib.org/library/Enc/ Monetarism.html. Retrieved 27 June 2010.

Miller, Rich (2008-01-28). "Global Recession Risk Grows as U.S. `Damage' Spreads". Bloomberg.com.

Mishkin, Frederic S. (2004), *The Economics of Money, Banking, and Financial Markets,* Boston: Addison-Wesley, p. 517.

Mishkin, Frederic S. (1995). *The Economics of Money, Banking, and Financial Markets*, New York, Harper Collins.

Moore, Stephen (2003-02-28). "Think Twice About Gregory Mankiw". *National Review*.

Nelson, Edward (2007). "Milton Friedman and U.S. Monetary History: 1961-2006". *Federal Reserve Bank of St. Louis Review* (89 (3)): 171. http:// research.stlouisfed.org/publications/review/07/05/ Nelson.pdf.

Nenovsky. N, (2007): "Exchange Rate and Inflation: France and Bulgaria in the Interwar Period and the Contribution of Albert Aftalion (1874-1956)". *Bulgarian National Bank,* (2006)

O'Sullivan, Arthur; Steven M. Sheffrin (2003). *Economics: Principles in Action*. Upper Saddle River, New Jersey 07458: Pearson Prentice Hall. pp. 330.

Olivei, Giovanni P. (2002). "Switzerland's Approach to Monetary Policy". *New England Economic Review* (Federal Reserve Bank of Boston) (Second Quarter): 57–60. http://www.bos.frb.org/economic/neer/neer2002/neer202l.pdf.

Pierro Sraffa (1932). "Dr. Hayek on Money and Capital". *Economic Journal (reprinted in Hayek 1995)* 42 (March): 42–53.

Plosser, Charles I. (1989). "Understanding real business cycles". *Journal of Economic Perspectives* 3: 51–77.

Quiggin, John (15 October 2010). "Five Zombie Economic Ideas That Refuse to Dies". Foreign Policy.

Quinn, Stephen; Roberds, William (2006). "An Economic Explanation of the Early Bank of Amsterdam, Debasement, Bills of Exchange, and the Emergence of the First Central Bank", Federal Reserve Bank of Atlanta, Working Paper 2006-13

Robert J. Shiller (2009-06-07). "Why Home Prices May Keep Falling". *New York Times*, June 6, 2009.

Rogoff, Kenneth (1985). "The Optimal Commitment to an Intermediate Monetary Target", *Quarterly Journal of Economics* 100, pp. 1169–1189.

Romer, David (1993). "The New Keynesian Synthesis". *The Journal of Economic Perspectives* 7 (1): 5-22.

Samuelson, Paul A. (Sep 1964). "Theory and Realism: A Reply". *The American Economic Review* (American Economic Association): 736–739.

Sargent, Thomas J. (2008). "Rational Expectations". The Concise Encyclopedia of Economics. Library of

Economics and Liberty. http://www.econlib.org/library/Enc/RationalExpectations.html.

Sawamiphakdi, D. (1989). *The economic impact of the demand for Arkansas tourism.* Doctoral dissertation, University of Arkansas.

Scheiber, Noam (2004-04-08). "Can Greg Mankiw Survive Politics?". *The New Republic.*

Shiller, Robert J. (2009-01-27). "WSJ-Robert Shiller-Animal Spirits Depend on Trust". Online.wsj.com.

Shiskin, Julius (1974-12-01). "The Changing Business Cycle". *New York Times*: p. 222.

Siegel, Jeremy J. (2002). Stocks for the Long Run: The Definitive Guide to Financial Market Returns and Long-Term Investment Strategies, 3rd, New York: McGraw-Hill, 388. ISBN 9780071370486

Siverts, Leif E (1988). *Modeling regional economic change at the county level: an IMPLAN application.* Doctoral dissertation, Michigan State University.

Skidelsky, Robert (2003). *John Maynard Keynes, 1883-1946.* New York: Penguin Books.

Snowdon, Brian and Vane, Howard R., (2005). *Modern Macroeconomics: Its Origin, Development and Current State.* Edward Elgar Publishing.

Snowdon, Brian, and Howard R. Vane, ed. (2002). *An Encyclopedia of Macroeconomics*, Description & scroll to Contents-preview links.

Snowdon, Brian; Howard Vane (2005). *Modern Macroeconomics.* Cheltenham: E. Elgar.

Stynes, D. J. and Susan, I. S. (1991). *The impacts of the Grand Traverse Resort on the local community.* East Lansing, MI: Department of Park, Recreation and Tourism Resources, Michigan State University.

Stynes, D. J., Zheng, J. and Stewart, S. (1995). *Seasonal homes in Michigan.* East Lansing, MI: Department of Park, Recreation and Tourism Resources, Michigan State University.

Sullivan, arthur; Steven M. Sheffrin (2003). *Economics: Principles in action*. Upper Saddle River, New Jersey 07458: Pearson Prentice Hall, p. 387.

Summers, Lawrence H. (1986). "Some Skeptical Observations on Real Business Cycle Theory". *Federal Reserve Bank of Minneapolis Quarterly Review* 10 (Fall): 23–27.

Susmianto, A. (1995). *Recreational expenditures in Gede Pangrango National Park and their regional economic impacts (Indonesia)*. Master's thesis, Michigan State University.

Tobin, J. (1992). "Voodoo curse". *Harvard International Review* 14 (4): 10.

Vaitilingam, Romesh (17 September 2009). "Recession Britain: New ESRC report on the impact of recession on people's jobs, businesses and daily lives". Economic and *Social Research Council*.

Vasudevan, Ramaa, "What is the relation between inflation and unemployment?", in *Dollars & Sense*, September/October 2006.

Vienneau, Robert L. "On Labour Demand and Equilibria of the Firm", *Manchester School*, V. 73, N. 5 (Sep. 2005): 612-619.

Wanniski, Jude (1978). *The Way the World Works: How Economies Fail—and Succeed*. New York: Basic Books.

Wanniski, Jude (1994). "Karl Marx Revisited". http://www.polyconomics.com/essays/esy-940124.htm.

Warsh, David (2006), *Knowledge and the Wealth of Nations,* Norton.

White, Lawrence H. (2008), "The research program of Austrian economics", *Advances in Austrian Economics* (Emerald Group Publishing Limited): 20.

White, William (April 2006) (PDF). *Is Price Stability Enough?*. Bank for International Settlements.

Woodford, Michael (2009). "Convergence in Macroeconomics:Elements of the New Synthesis". *American Economic Journal: Macroeconomics 1* (1): 267–79.

Woods, Jr., Thomas (2007). "22:Did Capitalism Cause the Great Depression?". *33 Questions about American History You're Not Supposed to Ask*. New York: Crown Forum. pp. 174–179.

Wright, Jonathan H., The Yield Curve and Predicting Recessions (March 2006). *FEDs Working Paper* No. 2006-7.

Index